CITYSPOTS
VIENNA

WHAT'S IN YOUR GUIDEBOOK?

Independent authors Impartial up-to-date information from our travel experts who meticulously source local knowledge.

Experience Thomas Cook's 165 years in the travel industry and guidebook publishing enriches every word with expertise you can trust.

Travel know-how Contributions by thousands of staff around the globe, each one living and breathing travel.

Editors Travel-publishing professionals, pulling everything together to craft a perfect blend of words, pictures, maps and design.

You, the traveller We deliver a practical, no-nonsense approach to information, geared to how you really use it.

● *Schönbrunn Palace (see page 49)*

CITYSPOTS
VIENNA

Kerry Walker

Thomas Cook

Written by Kerry Walker
Original photography by Caroline Jones
Front cover photography (Belvedere Palaces) © Fantuz
Olimpio/www.4cornersimages.com
Series design based on an original concept by Studio 183 Limited

Produced by Cambridge Publishing Management Limited
Project Editor: Rebecca McKie
Layout: Julie Crane
Maps: PC Graphics
Transport map: © Communicarta Limited

Published by Thomas Cook Publishing
A division of Thomas Cook Tour Operations Limited
Company Registration No. 1450464 England
PO Box 227, Unit 18, Coningsby Road
Peterborough PE3 8SB, United Kingdom
email: books@thomascook.com
www.thomascookpublishing.com
+ 44 (0) 1733 416477
ISBN: 978-184157-754-8

First edition © 2007 Thomas Cook Publishing
Text © 2007 Thomas Cook Publishing
Maps © 2007 Thomas Cook Publishing
Series Project Editor: Kelly Anne Pipes
Project Editor: Karen Fitzpatrick
Production/DTP: Steven Collins

Printed and bound in Spain by GraphyCems

CONTENTS

INTRODUCING VIENNA

Introduction...................................8
When to go 10
Vienna Ball season 14
History..16
Lifestyle 18
Culture..20

MAKING THE MOST OF VIENNA

Shopping......................................24
Eating & drinking...................27
Entertainment & nightlife...31
Sport & relaxation 34
Accommodation 37
The best of Vienna.................42
Something for nothing 46
When it rains.............................48
On arrival....................................50

THE CITY OF VIENNA

The city centre.........................60
Neubau...76
Leopoldstadt &
   Landstrasse 90

OUT OF TOWN

Wienerwald............................104
The Wachau Valley...............117

PRACTICAL INFORMATION

Directory...................................128
Emergencies 138

INDEX 140

MAPS

Vienna 52
Vienna transport map 56
The city centre.........................62
Neubau...78
Leopoldstadt &
   Landstrasse.........................92
Vienna region.........................106

SYMBOLS KEY

The following symbols are used throughout this book:

ⓐ address ⓣ telephone ⓦ website address ⓔ email
ⓛ opening times ⓝ public transport connections ⓘ important

The following symbols are used on the maps:

𝒊	information office	O	city
✈	airport	O	large town
✚	hospital	○	small town
🛡	police station	═	motorway
🚌	bus station	━	main road
🚆	railway station		minor road
Ⓜ	metro	—	railway
✝	cathedral		
❶	numbers denote featured cafés & restaurants		

Hotels and restaurants are graded by approximate price
as follows:
£ budget ££ mid-range £££ expensive

▶ *The Rathaus (Vienna City Hall)*

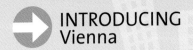

Introduction

A jewel box stuffed with Habsburg treasures and avant-garde architecture, Vienna (or Wien, to give it its Austrian name) offers the perfect combination of romantic nostalgia and in-your-face innovation with its whirl of frothy rococo palaces, world-class galleries, great shopping and grand concert halls. If you want to discover the city of the Blue Danube, the former epicentre of an empire and the home of the mammoth MuseumsQuartier cultural complex, waltz this way.

Looking as though it has stepped straight out of a fairy tale by the Brothers Grimm, Vienna has thrilled visitors for centuries. Trams rumble around the tree-fringed Ringstrasse boulevard, horse-drawn traps pull up in front of Gothic giant St Stephen's Cathedral and the Prater's Ferris wheel turns by day and twinkles by night. It won't be long before you start to share the city's obsession with coffee and sticky cakes and its passion for culture.

While classic highlights like the Imperial Palace and Belvedere Gallery still top most must-see lists, a growing crop of funky boutiques, offbeat galleries, new-wave restaurants and quirky hotels are giving the centre a millennial kick. If you haven't been for a while, you're in for a surprise! Laid-back and lively, Vienna's 1.6 million residents know how to have fun, with blurry-eyed nights in brewpubs and bopping in clubs by the Danube Canal keeping the vibe playful.

After you've discovered the heart of the city, Vienna's wild backyard beckons. A mere stone's throw to the west, the Wienerwald has plenty of back-to-nature pleasures tucked up its green sleeve, from precipitous medieval castles set on limestone crags to sublime Benedictine abbeys and effervescent spas. You can graze for days on the riches of the World Heritage Wachau Valley, just an hour from the city, where steep vines tumble down to the Danube. Dramatic cityscapes and nature trails, all-night parties and pin-drop peace: the Austrian capital has got the lot!

⬥ Get fantastic views from the Riesenrad Ferris wheel in Prater Park

When to go

SEASONS & CLIMATE

Vienna has a temperate climate with sunny summers peaking at around 25°C (77°F) – the time to come for open-air festivals and late-night partying. In winter, wrap up warm for sub-zero climes (sometimes plummeting to –10°C (14°F)), which often bring a generous sprinkling of snow. With mild temperatures hovering between 10° and 15°C (50° and 59°F), spring is when the capital's parks are at their best. Autumn brings fewer crowds and a final burst of colour in the woods fringing the city.

ANNUAL EVENTS

January
New Year's Day Concert in Vienna
Catch this world-famous New Year's concert with the Philharmonic Orchestra at Vienna Musikverein's Golden Hall.
ⓐ Boesendorfer Strasse 12 ⓣ 01 505 6525
ⓦ www.wienerphilharmoniker.at
Practitioners' Ball
Dress up to the nines to attend this sublime ball at the Hofburg Palace. ⓐ Kaisertor/Innerer Burghof ⓣ 01 51 501 1234
ⓦ www.aerzteball.at

February
Vienna Opera Ball
Sounds of Strauss, couples twirling across the floor and plenty of glamour and glitz. ⓐ Opernring 2 ⓣ 01 51 444 2613
ⓦ www.wiener-staatsoper.at ⓔ opernball@wiener-staatsoper.at

March/April
Schönbrunn Easter Fair
Stalls selling amazing eggs, tin toys and Easter wreaths, plus Easter egg hunts and other activities. ❸ Schönbrunner Schloss Strasse ❶ 01 81113 239 Ⓦ www.schoenbrunn.at

April
City Festival
Vienna leaps into spring with this three-day festival. From concerts and clowns to improvised theatre and parties, everything at this fun-fuelled event is free! ❶ 01 548 4800 Ⓦ www.stadtfestwien.at

May
Life Ball
Celebrities and supermodels raise funds for AIDS at this star-studded ball in City Hall. ❸ Rathausplatz ❶ 01 718 7700 Ⓦ www.lifeball.org ❸ information@lifeball.at

May–June
Vienna Festival
Culture vultures flock to this mammoth festival which features a string of theatre and music highlights. ❶ 01 589 2222 Ⓦ www.festwochen.at ❸ kartenbuero@festwochen.at

June
Danube Island Festival
Three-day festival of free open-air concerts and performances by local and international bands on the Danube's islands.

ⓐ Danube ⓣ 01 535 3535 ⓦ www.donauinselfest.at
ⓔ office@donauinselfest.at

June–July
Jazz Fest Wien (Vienna Jazz Festival)
Expect smooth jazz and big talent appearing at venues across
Vienna. ⓣ 01 712 4224 ⓦ www.viennajazz.org
ⓔ office@viennajazz.org

July–August
KlangBogen
This festival's world-class opera and classical performances are
magnets to music buffs. ⓐ Linke Wienzeile 6 ⓣ 01 427 17
ⓦ www.klangbogen.at ⓔ tickets@klangbogen.at

October
Viennale
Austria's biggest film festival keeps Vienna glued to big screens
across the city. ⓐ Siebensterngasse 2 ⓣ 01 526 59 47
ⓦ www.viennale.at ⓔ office@viennale.or.at

December
Christmas Market
Nibble on gingerbread and sip mulled wine beneath twinkling
trees on Rathausplatz at this 700-year-old festive market.
ⓐ Rathausplatz ⓣ 01 24 555 ⓦ www.christkindlmarkt.at
Imperial Ball
Ringing in the New Year and Vienna's ball season, the Imperial
Ball is a grand occasion at the palace. ⓐ Kaisertor/Innerer

Burghof ☎ 01 587 36 6623 🌐 www.hofburg.com
✉ kaiserball@hofburg.com

PUBLIC HOLIDAYS

New Year's Day 1 January
Epiphany 6 January
Easter Monday March/April
National Holiday 1 May
Ascension Day May
Whit Monday June
Corpus Christi June
Assumption August

National Holiday
  26 October
All Saints' Day 1 November
Conception 8 December
Christmas Day
  25 December
Boxing Day 26 December

🔺 *Join the hordes at the Rathausplatz Christmas market*

Vienna Ball season

Whirling through more than 200 balls during the *Fasching* period (carnival) from New Year to late February, Vienna certainly knows how to beat the winter blues with a little sparkle and Strauss. In the birthplace of the waltz, the ball season is firmly rooted in Austrian culture. The boggling decorations, fancy footwork and free-flowing champagne will sweep you off your feet.

⬤ *Couples glide across the floor at the Practitioners' Ball*

The balls range from intimate dos to incredibly grand affairs held at the stately Hofburg Palace. Dressing up is usually a must – ties and tails for men and ankle-length dresses for women. If you want to join the fun, but don't have a tux or taffeta ball gown handy, there are a number of places in town which rent formal wear. Those with two left feet can take expert tips to polish their foxtrot, polka and waltz with dance lessons before the event.

Dazzling in their finery, Vienna's high society and other mortals lucky enough to have tickets turn out for the biggies, including the Imperial Ball which rings in New Year at the Hofburg Palace, the elegant Practitioners' Ball, the Philharmonic Ball, the Kaffeesiederball staged by the capital's coffee houses and, perhaps most famous of all, the sublime Opera Ball where pink carnations rain down when the orchestra plays *The Blue Danube*. Quirky additions feature the bizarre Wallflower Ball (dress code: drab) and the Ball of Bad Taste where the music and clothes are truly awful.

Whether you want to mingle with the glitterati, follow the rhythm of the polonaise or slip into one of the wackier events, you'll need to book tickets well in advance (the tourist office provides details). Listen out for *Alles Waltzer*, your cue to dance.

🅐 Albertinaplatz/Maysedergasse 🕿 01 24 555 🅕 01 24 555 666 🅦 www.wien.info 🅔 info@wien.info 🕘 09.00–19.00 Mon–Sun

History

Baroque palaces, formal gardens, stately homes and world-class museums shape what was once the epicentre of the Habsburg Empire. While the capital is best known for its imperial clout, its road to success hasn't always been smooth. On the crossroads of trade routes between East and West, it was a melting pot of cultures and often a battlefield.

In 15 BC the Romans set up a military camp called Vindobona, laying the foundations of what would become Vienna. Things moved swiftly in the 10th century when Vienna bloomed into one of the biggest towns north of the Alps under the Babenburg clan and commerce flourished. It rose to prominence in the 12th century as the seat of dukes and emperors. The city walls were completed in 1200, built on the ransom the English paid to release their imprisoned king, Richard the Lionheart.

The Habsburgs took power in 1278, beginning their 640-year reign. During medieval times, the city continued to prosper and the University of Vienna was founded in 1365. Developments came to a temporary halt when Ottoman forces invaded Austria and besieged Vienna in 1529, then again in 1683. Both attempts failed and the Turks were defeated with Polish and German help.

Vienna boomed in the 17th and 18th centuries – palaces like Prince Eugene of Savoy's Belvedere sprouted up and the aristocracy poured pots of money into creating an impressive cityscape. Great minds like Mozart, Haydn, Beethoven and, in later years, Schubert and Strauss were drawn to the capital of classical music. But 1898 was marked by mourning when the country's beloved Empress Elisabeth (Sisi) was assassinated in Geneva.

In the wake of World War I, the Austro-Hungarian Empire collapsed in 1918. In 1938, Austria was annexed to Hitler's Germany and Vienna became a provincial capital in the Third Reich. The city's Jewish residents were forced into exile or murdered and by the end of World War II in 1945 Vienna had been morally drained and physically devastated.

Following ten years of Allied occupation, the Austrian Independence Treaty was signed in 1955 and the republic achieved sovereign status. In 1979 the UN City was opened, Austria became an EU member in 1995 and Vienna's historic centre was designated a UNESCO World Heritage Site in 2001. With its brand-new MuseumsQuartier and the city's pride in hosting the Euro 2008 finals, Vienna is very much on the up.

▲ The Johann Strauss statue in the Stadtpark

Lifestyle

Traditional, trendy and everything in between, today's Vienna dishes up quite a few surprises. Yes, you'll find the parks and palaces basking in imperial splendour, but scratch the surface to unearth a growing crop of trendy lounge bars in Spittelberg, kooky boutiques in the MuseumsQuartier and a hot electronic music scene on the Danube Canal's banks. Skipping from Habsburg treasures to hedonism, and from old-style coffee houses to cocktails in glass-walled bars, Vienna is a master in the art of enjoyment.

The Viennese are a pleasure-seeking bunch, as the capital's knot of sleek boutiques, plush restaurants and chichi bars confirms. Great thinkers, dreamers and coffee drinkers, the laid-back locals love to relax and hate to rush. They even have a word to sum up this easy life – *Gemütlichkeit*, or snugness. Fit in by dwelling over an alfresco lunch, philosophising over a bottomless cup of coffee and watching the world go by in the Prater. Unlike other capitals, this one simply doesn't do hectic.

Genuinely friendly when they come out of their formal shell, the Viennese are polite and happy to help. Most speak good English, although a smattering of German will go a long way if you're planning on exploring districts away from the centre. Life in Vienna revolves around having a good time, which could involve taking in an exhibition, going to a concert, or taking a stroll in the woods. From Michelin-starred restaurants to picnicking in the park, this capital enjoys the high life but has its feet firmly on the ground – pretty but unpretentious, urban but with the countryside close at hand.

A lively student population of around 130,000 breathes new life into the city and makes sure it rocks by night. With a glut of cheery hostels around Mariahilfer Strasse, plus cheap-and-cheerful cafés and brewpubs clustering around the centre, a visit to Vienna doesn't have to cost a fortune. Seamlessly merging new and old, the capital is successfully propelling itself into the 21st century with a fresh take on art and shopping around the MuseumsQuartier, but has by no means lost sight of its rich tradition.

◆ *Unwind over coffee at Café Central*

Culture

Culture in the Austrian capital is alive and kicking. You won't have to search hard to immerse yourself in palatial museums crammed with masterpieces, snug coffee houses where locals bury their heads in books, and districts stacked with baroque and Biedermeier houses. An intriguing mishmash of old and new, Vienna is up to its neck in imperial riches, but embracing innovation with open arms.

In the city that inspired maestros like Beethoven, Mahler, Mozart, Schubert and Strauss, it's little wonder the Viennese take classical music seriously. The capital's greatest glory is the Vienna State Opera, staging some of the world's finest opera and ballet. Other big draws include chamber music at the Wiener Konzerthaus, the Vienna Philharmonic Orchestra performing at the Musikverein's resplendent Golden Hall, and the Volksoper for musicals and operettas.

With 50 venues and a range of shows which runs from avant-garde plays to small-scale productions and cabaret, Vienna has a thriving theatre scene. Avid theatregoers should try to get tickets for a performance at the 19th-century Burgtheater, which stages a variety of old favourites and new interpretations in an opulent setting. The Volkstheater Wien specialises in contemporary performances, while the English Theatre in Josefstadt has a mix of English-speaking musicals, comedies and plays.

Unrivalled in the art department, Vienna is a kaleidoscope palette of Old Masters and new talent. Start off at the Hofburg, which showcases glittering jewels and Biedermeier portraits, then head over to the Albertina, with its riot of Rembrandts, Picassos and Warhols, or graze on the Kunsthistorisches Museum's riches, which include works by Velázquez and Caravaggio. Design reaches a peak at the Museum of Applied Arts (MAK), which houses precious Wiener Werkstätte pieces. Visit the Upper Belvedere for great Impressionist works and a peerless Klimt collection, or see Hundertwasser's colours make a Secessionist splash at KunstHaus Wien.

⏶ *The Upper Belvedere contains some of the best art in Vienna (see page 97)*

Adding a modern twist to Vienna's art offerings, the MuseumsQuartier is one of the ten largest cultural complexes in the world, spanning 45,000 sq m (54,000 sq yds). Take a trip to the cube-shaped Leopold Museum, which houses an impressive collection of Egon Schiele paintings, or the Kunsthalle Wien, where contemporary art comes to the fore. The monolithic Museum of Modern Art Ludwig Foundation thrusts you into the 20th century with works by Warhol, Magritte and Kandinsky. For music and dance with cutting edge, look no further than Halle E & G and Tanzquartier Wien.

AFTER-DARK ARTS

Get your nocturnal cultural kicks when Vienna's top museums stay open late once a week. After-hours art draws culture vultures to biggies like the Albertina (open until 21.00 on Wednesdays), the Museum of Modern Art Ludwig Foundation, the Leopold Museum (open until 21.00 on Thursdays) and the latest of them all, the MAK (open until 24.00 on Tuesdays).

❯ *The vibrant street scene around Stephansplatz*

Shopping

Bring an extra-large suitcase, as Vienna has fantastic shops. The savvy Viennese even came up with the idea of the coffee house to give shoppers' feet a break. The Austrian capital has some 20,000 shops, ranging from boho boutiques to baroque antiques emporia. So whether you're after high fashion, dainty porcelain or chocolates to eat on the way home, you're in the right place.

Shopping hours are generally 09.00–18.30 Monday to Friday and 09.00–17.00 Saturday. Many shops stay open till 21.00 on Thursdays or Fridays. Souvenir shops, bakeries, and station and airport shops open on Sundays.

Shopping streets

Designer labels dangle in the boutiques lining Kärntner Strasse, Graben and Kohlmarkt, where names like Armani and Tiffany & Co rub shoulders. On the streets fanning out from Stephansplatz, you'll find everything from the latest Viennese styles to confectionery and crystal. Look out for antiques on Dorotheergasse and Stallburggasse, or make for Mariahilfer Strasse for wall-to-wall high-street fashion.

Shopping malls

Find slinky shoes and cosmetics in the Ringstrasse Gallerien, or browse 50 shops under one roof at department store Steffl – take the glass elevator to the top for far-reaching views over Vienna.

King of the malls, the giant Gasometer in the 11th district houses big stores, snack bars and a 12-screen cinema.

USEFUL SHOPPING PHRASES

What time do the shops open/close?
Um wieviel Uhr öffnen/schließen die Geschäfte?
Oom veefeel oor erffnen/shleessen dee geshefter?

How much is this?
Wieviel kostet das?
Veefeel kostet das?

Can I try this on?
Kann ich das anprobieren?
Can ikh das anprobeeren?

My size is ...
Ich habe Größe ...
Ikh haber grerser ...

I'll take this one, thank you
Ich nehme das, danke schön
Ikh neymer das, danker shern

This is too large/too small/too expensive
Es ist zu groß/zu klein/zu teuer
Es ist tsu gross/tsu kline/tsu toyer

Something unique

A few steps from the Naschmarkt, Freihausviertel is packed with pocket-sized galleries and kooky boutiques selling retro furniture, handmade ethnic jewellery and one-off artworks. For vintage fashion, ultra-modern gadgets and 60s psychedelia, head to Neubaugasse, Kirchengasse and the MuseumsQuartier's quartier21.

Markets

The pick of the bunch is Naschmarkt in the 4th district, where stalls are piled high with fresh fruit, colourful spices, huge cheeses and barrels of glistening olives from Monday to Friday and second-hand gems at Saturday's flea market. There's also a plethora of cafés where you can join the locals for sushi or espresso. For fresh produce and a laid-back feel, make for Karmelitermarkt and Rochusmarkt.

Best buys

Take home Augarten porcelain (well wrapped of course!), multi-coloured Hundertwasser postcards, a hand-painted Lipizzaner stallion to decorate your own palace and candied violets from Demel for a lingering taste of Vienna.

⬥ *Mariahilfer Strasse is the focal point for high street shopping*

Eating & drinking

Vienna serves fine food at affordable prices compared with other capitals. There are thousands of places to eat, from sleek tapas and sushi bars to elegant Michelin-starred restaurants and the ubiquitous *würstelstände* (sausage stands). Whether it's to be a cavernous brewpub with homebrews and tasty snacks or a wood-panelled wine tavern, this city defies anyone to go hungry.

Dining districts

The centre's eateries are a mouth-watering fusion of Viennese classics and world flavours. Tucked down the streets fanning out from Stephansplatz are relaxed trattorias and gourmet haunts, ultra-modern sushi bars and snug cafés serving cheap and tasty fare. There are some great places around MuseumsQuartier where you can eat surrounded by striking architecture. For alfresco dining, head for the Prater's clutch of laid-back cafés and restaurants.

Food markets

In the Wieden district, Vienna's vibrant Naschmarkt is an attraction in its own right. Alongside the mounds of fresh fruit are huge cheeses, seafood, olives and racks of colourful spices. You can spend hours wandering from stall to stall, popping into cafés for an espresso and eating your way around the world at hole-in-the-wall restaurants dishing up everything from falafel and curries to sushi and stir-fries fresh from the wok.

Picnic spots

Peppered with parks and gardens, Vienna is the ideal place for a picnic when the sun shines. Fill your basket with local specialities and head for the Volksgarten to rest beside the fountains and roses, or lay your blanket down by the water's edge on the Danube Island.

Local specialities

A melting pot of Austrian, Bohemian, Hungarian and Balkan flavours, Viennese cuisine is flavoursome and hearty. Traditional fare includes *Wiener Schnitzel* (breaded veal cutlet), Hungarian-

● *The area around Naschmarkt is full of cafés and restaurants*

COFFEE CULTURE

A far cry from the quick caffeine fix, Vienna likes to linger and savour coffee at its leisure. From old-world giants like Sacher and Prückel decked out with chandeliers to shabby chic cafés with creaking floors, the Viennese coffee house is an institution where locals come to chat, philosophise, write, read the daily papers and enjoy concerts.

Some coffee houses feature 20 different varieties, including *Grosse Schwarzer* (double espresso), *Fiaker* (strong black coffee laced with kirsch and topped with whipped cream and a cherry) and *Maria Theresia* (mocha with orange liqueur and whipped cream).

style *Fiakergulasch* (beef goulash with plenty of paprika), *Klare Rindsuppe* (beef broth) with *Griessknockerl* (semolina dumplings) and *Tafelspitz* (braised beef). Try the home-grown Riesling and Grüner Veltiner wines, or sample local beers like 7 Stern Bräu and Salm Bräu in brewery pubs. The sweet-toothed Viennese always save room for dessert. Tuck into flaky apple strudel, *Kaiserschmarren* (sugared pancakes with raisins) and *Powidltaschen* (potato puffs filled with plum jam).

Tipping

Many of Vienna's restaurants and cafés include a service charge in the bill, but it's normal to leave a tip if you were pleased with the service. Locals usually tip around 5–10 per cent. In Austria, it's standard practice to tip waiters and waitresses when paying the bill, not by leaving the money on the table.

USEFUL DINING PHRASES

I would like a table for ... people
Ein Tisch für ... Personen, bitte
Ine teesh foor ... perzohnen, bitter

Waiter/waitress!
Herr Ober/Fräulein, bitte!
Hair ohber/froyline, bitter!

May I have the bill, please?
Die Rechnung, bitte?
Dee rekhnung, bitter?

I am a vegetarian. Does this contain meat?
Ich bin Vegetarier (Vegetarierin fem.). Enthält das hier Fleisch?
Ish bin veggetaareer (veggetaareerin). Enthelt dass heer flyshe?

Where is the toilet (restroom) please?
Wo sind die Toiletten, bitte?
Voo zeent dee toletten, bitter?

I would like a cup of/two cups of/another coffee/tea
Eine Tasse/Zwei Tassen/noch eine Tasse Kaffee/Tee, bitte
Ikh merkhter iner tasser/tsvy tassen kafey/tey, bitter

I would like a beer/two beers, please
Ein Bier/Zwei Biere, bitte
Ine beer/tsvy beerer, bitter

PRICE RATING
The restaurant price guides used in this book indicate the approximate cost of a three-course meal for one person, excluding drinks, at the time of writing.
£ up to €20   ££ €20–€35   £££ over €40

Entertainment & nightlife

Vienna twinkles by night, as the Hofburg shines and the capital's bars and restaurants glow. Whether you're looking for a relaxed pub to chill out or a sleek lounge bar to shake your booty to hiphop, this 24-hour city comes up with the goods.

A mixed bag of hip and traditional, Vienna has an after-dark scene to match every season. Summer in the city spells late nights in alfresco bars and beer gardens, where night owls spill out onto pocket-sized terraces and inner courtyards. As the nights get colder, the Viennese head indoors to sip fruity Rieslings in snug wine taverns and unwind in wood-panelled cafés oozing musty charm.

There are few cities in the world that can match Vienna when it comes to culture. The capital steps effortlessly from opera to classical music, theatre, live jazz and cabaret. To book tickets in advance, contact the venue direct or try Vienna Ticket Office, which covers major festivals, gigs and performances. ⓐ Kärntner Strasse 51 ⓣ 01 513 1111 ⓦ www.viennaticketoffice.com ⓔ info@viennaticketoffice.com ⓛ 09.00–18.50 daily

Pubs and bars

Within the Ring, the so-called 'Bermuda Triangle' appeals with a glut of lively bars, cafés and clubs vying for your custom. The centre's main drag, this triangle of streets around St Ruprecht's Church is the place to come for wall-to-wall entertainment and an eclectic crowd who come to see and be seen. Top addresses to seek out include First Floor for its arm-long cocktail list, Krah

Krah for brilliant beers and Absolut Bar for chilled vodka that packs a punch.

Vienna's alternative pulse beats around the hip Gürtel area, where you can party to urban and electro beats in bars with industrial edge beneath the railway arches. Hot spots where bright young things hang out include the glass-fronted B72 and spacey Babu. Make for nearby Spittelberg, where creaking pubs, delectable cocktail lounges and vibrant bars huddle in a web of narrow streets.

Clubs

Clubbers dance till dawn by the Danube and the Prater peps up the late-night offer with clubs like Fluc, where DJs and live concerts keep partygoers on their toes. In the centre, beautiful people share the dance floor at Volksgarten overlooking the Imperial Palace, while Flex gets loud pumping out drum'n'bass and techno tunes.

GOODNESS GRAPE-CIOUS

Keep an eye out for Vienna's *Heurigen*, traditional taverns serving only locally produced wines together with tasty buffet snacks and occasionally Austrian folk music. You'll know you've found one of these quintessential Viennese haunts when you see a sprig of pine branches above the door and a sign saying *Ausg'steckt*, which means it's open for custom. Most wine taverns lie on the city's fringes in the 16th, 19th and 21st districts. Come to taste the grape and drink in the laid-back atmosphere.

Performing arts

As night falls, Vienna's stages light up with stars. Culture vultures catch contemporary and classic performances at the sumptuous National Theatre, and opera, ballet and classical music at the grand 19th-century Vienna State Opera. If you want something a bit less mainstream, the MuseumsQuartier's Halle E & G and Tanzquartier Wien are at the crest of cutting-edge performing arts.

Entertainment listings

Hauptstadt ⓦ www.hauptstadt.at gives the lowdown on Vienna's nightlife, including clubs, concerts, cinema and cabaret, while online magazine Falter has the latest listings ⓦ www.falter.at

🔺 The Red Room (see page 75): one of Vienna's hottest nightclubs

Sport & relaxation

SPECTATOR SPORTS
Football
Footy fans should try to catch a match at the state-of-the-art Ernst-Happel-Stadion, Austria's largest stadium and home to the national football team. ⓐ Meiereistrasse 7 ⓣ 01 728 0854 Ⓝ Tram: 21 Meiereistrasse

PARTICIPATION SPORTS
Walking & cycling
Dappled with expansive parks and gardens, Vienna is made for walking and cycling. Wander the leafy Prater and the Belvedere's alpine gardens, or hop on your bike to explore the marked trails which crisscross the nearby Wienerwald.

Swimming
In summer, locals cool off with a dip in the open-air Badeschiff barge on the Danube Canal, featuring a 30-m (98-ft) swimming pool. ⓐ Wiesingerstrasse 6 ⓣ 01 513 0744 Ⓦ www.badeschiff.at Ⓝ U-Bahn: U1 Schwedenplatz. Admission charge

GET YOUR SKATES ON!
Vienna gets ready to roll every Friday night from May to September, as skaters gather at Heldenplatz to flit through the city's streets. Join this fun, free event for a whirlwind tour of the sights by night. Ⓦ www.fridaynightskating.at

○ *Rollerskating is a popular pastime in Vienna*

Bungee jumping

Daredevils dangle upside-down from the 152-m (499-ft) Danube Tower. The world's highest jump from a tower, this nerve-splintering experience is available from April to October. ⓐ Donauturmstrasse 4 ⓣ 01 263 3572 ⓦ www.donauturm.at ⓝ Bus: 20B Danube Tower

RELAXATION

Leisure

Water is never far away in Vienna. When the weather gets warm, the Danube Island attracts crowds to its bays, tree-fringed promenade and waterfront cafés. Come here to swim, stroll, skate or hire a boat. There's even a nudist area if you dare to bare! ⓝ U-Bahn: U1 Donauinsel

Spa

Unwind in Oberlaa thermal baths with 36°C (97°F) waters, pummelling massage points and a Feng Shui-inspired sauna complex. ⓐ Kurbadstrasse 14 ⓣ 01 680 099 600 ⓦ www.oberlaa.at ⓛ 08.45–22.00 Mon–Sat, 07.45–22.00 Sun ⓝ U-Bahn: U1 Reumannplatz. Admission charge

Hammam

Pamper yourself with a steam in this oriental-style hammam, a stone's throw away from the MuseumsQuartier. ⓐ Rahlgasse 5 ⓣ 01 585 66 4520 ⓦ www.auxgazelles.at ⓛ 12.00–22.00 Mon–Sat, closed Sun ⓝ U-Bahn: U2 Museumsquartier. Admission charge

Accommodation

From cheap-and-cheerful backpacker digs with a 24-hour party vibe to neat-and-petite guesthouses with bags of charm, Vienna has something to suit every style and pocket.

> **PRICE RATING**
> The ratings below indicate the approximate cost of a room for two people for one night.
> £ under €65   ££ €65–€120   £££ €120–€180

Campsites

Camping Neue Donau £ Pitch a tent at this peaceful site near the Prater. Swim from nearby bays or cycle miles of riverside trails. Facilities include a shop, barbecue area, internet access and bike rental. ❸ Am Kleehäufel
❶ 01 202 4010 ❻ www.wiencamping.at
ⓔ camping.neuedonau@verkehrsbuero.at ❹ Apr–Sept, closed Oct–Mar ❻ U-Bahn: U3 Stephansplatz; Bus: 91A

Camping Wien Süd £ Set in former palace gardens, this family-friendly site near Lake Brunn is surrounded by woods and meadows. Campers can use the barbecue area, playground and communal kitchen. ❸ Breitenfurter Strasse 269 ❶ 01 867 3649
❻ www.wiencamping.at ❹ May–Sept, closed Oct–Apr
❻ U-Bahn: U6 Siebenhirten; Bus: 62A

Hostels

Hostel Ruthensteiner £ A family affair, this cosy hostel three minutes' walk from Westbahnhof has a leafy courtyard, barbecue area, communal kitchen, free lockers and high-speed internet access. ⓐ Robert Hamerlinggasse 24 ⓣ 01 893 4202 ⓦ www.hostelruthensteiner.com
ⓔ info@hostelruthensteiner.com ⓝ U-Bahn: U3 Westbahnhof

Jugendherberge Myrthengasse £ This modern hostel near the MuseumsQuartier offers clean two- to six-bed dorms, with an inner courtyard, cable TV in the lobby and internet access. Prices include a good buffet breakfast. ⓐ Myrthengasse 7
ⓣ 01 523 6316 ⓦ www.oejhv.or.at ⓔ hostel@chello.at
ⓝ U-Bahn: U3 Neubaugasse

Wombat's City Hostel 'The Lounge' £ Voted the world's cleanest hostel, these central Aussie-style digs offer spacious dorms all with own shower. Enjoy a free welcome drink and handy stuff like lockers, laundry, kitchen and internet access. Party in the soundproofed basement bar. ⓐ Mariahilfer Strasse 137
ⓣ 01 897 2336 ⓕ 01 897 2577 ⓦ www.wombats-hostels.com
ⓔ office@wombats-vienna.at ⓝ U-Bahn: U3, U6 Westbahnhof

Guesthouses

Pension Hargita £ Expect a warm welcome at this 2-star Neubau guesthouse. The squeaky clean, light-filled rooms are decked out in cheery yellows and blues. ⓐ Andreasgasse 1/8
ⓣ 01 526 1928 ⓦ www.hargita.at ⓔ pension@hargita.at
ⓝ U-Bahn: U3 Zieglergasse

Pension Kraml £ Close to Mariahilfer Strasse, this elegant 19th-century townhouse set around a courtyard scores points for its large, quiet rooms and substantial buffet breakfast. The comfy rooms in earthy tones have wood floors, huge windows and all mod cons. ⓐ Brauergasse 5 ⓣ 01 587 8588 ⓦ www.pensionkraml.at ⓔ pension.kraml@chello.at ⓝ U-Bahn: U3 Zieglergasse

Pension Mozart £ Turn-of-the-century hotel near the Opera House, with high-ceilinged rooms and nice touches like chandeliers, pot plants and rocking chairs. The hearty breakfast

△ *Wallow in 5-star luxury at the Grand Hotel Wien*

comes recommended. ⓐ Theobaldgasse 15 ⓣ 01 587 8505
ⓦ www.pension-mozart.at ⓔ pension.mozart@chello.at
ⓝ U-Bahn: U3 Neubaugasse

Pension Reimer £ A great choice for the price, this art nouveau
guesthouse near the MuseumsQuartier has Viennese charm
and 14 attractive rooms. ⓐ Kirchengasse 18 ⓣ 01 523 6162
ⓦ www.pension-reimer.com ⓔ pension-reimer.com@aon.at
ⓝ U-Bahn: U3 Neubaugasse

Pharmador ££ An intimate hotel set round a pretty courtyard,
Pharmador offers smart rooms with cable TV, comfy beds
and minibar. Guests enjoy free parking and a yummy organic
buffet breakfast. ⓐ Schottenfeldgasse 39 ⓣ 01 523 5317
ⓦ www.pensionpharmador.at ⓝ U-Bahn: U3 Zieglergasse

Suzanne ££ The rooms at this 19th-century guesthouse offer a
touch of old-world grandeur with their high ceilings, antique
furniture and chandeliers. ⓐ Walfischgasse 4 ⓣ 01 513 2507
ⓦ www.pension-suzanne.at ⓔ info@pension-suzanne.at
ⓝ U-Bahn: U4 Karlsplatz/Oper

Hotels
Hotel Praterstern £ This recently renovated hotel near the Prater
offers excellent value. The wood-floored rooms in crisp whites
and blues have internet access. Unwind in the tranquil garden.
ⓐ Mayergasse 6 ⓣ 01 214 0123 ⓦ www.hotelpraterstern.at
ⓔ hotelpraterstern@aon.at ⓝ U-Bahn: U1 Praterstern

Hotel Kugel ££ This little gem of a hotel has snug rooms with canopy beds, satellite TV and minibar. The friendly staff will help you plan your stay. Prices include a buffet breakfast. ⓐ Siebensterngasse 43 ⓣ 01 523 3355 ⓦ www.hotelkugel.at ⓔ office@hotelkugel.at ⓝ U-Bahn: U3 Neubaugasse

Hotel Urania ££ Pick a room to match your personality at Vienna's quirkiest hotel. Each room has a theme – from baroque frescoes and Japanese minimalism to medieval chambers and wood-panelled alpine chalet designs. ⓐ Obere Weissgerberstrasse 7 ⓣ 01 713 1711 ⓦ www.hotel-urania.at ⓔ hotel.urania.@chello.at ⓝ U-Bahn: U1 Praterstern

Grand Hotel Wien £££ The Belle Epoque Grand Hotel has luxurious rooms and suites, two posh restaurants and a traditional café, all within a couple of minutes' walk of the Opera House. ⓐ Karntner Ring ⓣ 01 515 800 ⓦ www.jjwhotels.com ⓔ info@grandhotelwien.com ⓝ U-Bahn: U4 Oper

Hotel Rathaus Wein & Design £££ Everything at this sleek concept hotel revolves around wine – from wine cosmetics to wine cheese at breakfast. Minimalist chic sums up the Zen-inspired rooms and the all-important touches are there – from free welcome baskets to wine tasting. ⓐ Lange Gasse 13 ⓣ 01 400 1122 ⓦ www.hotel-rathaus-wien.at ⓔ office@hotel-rathaus-wien.at ⓝ U-Bahn: U3 Volkstheater

THE BEST OF VIENNA

With its staggering range of cultural attractions, happening bars and restaurants and a thriving club scene, this city has something for everyone.

TOP 10 ATTRACTIONS

- **Hofburg (Imperial Palace)** Admire lavish State Apartments and glittering crown jewels at this vast palace complex, once home to the Austrian Habsburgs (see page 60).

- **MuseumsQuartier** Explore one of the ten biggest cultural districts in the world, full of avant-garde architecture, modern art and funky boutiques (see pages 76–89).

- **Prater** The big wheel turns, carousels tinkle and rollercoasters offer eye-popping thrills at this massive funfair set in acres of parkland (see page 94).

- **Stephansdom (St Stephen's Cathedral)** Gaze up at the filigree spires and mosaic roof of Vienna's Gothic cathedral and climb to the top for giddy views (see page 64).

- **Staatsoper (Vienna State Opera)** See world-class opera and ballet at the 19th-century Opera House (see page 68).

- **Österreichische Galerie Belvedere (Belvedere Gallery)** Roam manicured gardens and see works by Monet at Prince Eugene of Savoy's rococo summer palace (see page 97).

- **Hundertwasserhaus** Curvy walls, twisting trees and shimmering mosaics characterise Friedensreich Hundertwasser's house (see page 91).

- **Sacher** Mmm is for mouth-watering *Sachertorte* chocolate cake baked according to a secret recipe at this historic Viennese coffee house (see page 71).

- **Kunsthistorisches Museum** Filled with Habsburg treasures including Old Master paintings by the likes of Caravaggio and Titian (see page 66).

- **Spittelberg** Old Vienna meets new in this hip district interlaced with narrow streets and dotted with Biedermeier houses, open-air cafés and kooky galleries (see page 76).

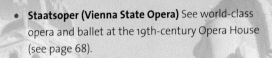
The Kunsthistorisches Museum

HALF-DAY: VIENNA IN A HURRY

A *Grosse Schwarzer* (double espresso) at Sacher fuels your morning's sightseeing. Whizz around the Ring on a tram to spot highlights including the City Hall and State Opera. Pause at the Imperial Palace to take a peek at the sumptuous State Apartments, then speed-shop in the smart boutiques peppering Kohlmarkt. Scale the tower of St Stephen's Cathedral for sweeping views over Vienna's rooftops.

1 DAY: TIME TO SEE A LITTLE MORE

Get up with the lark to sniff out the freshest produce at the colourful Naschmarkt, then make a beeline for the MuseumsQuartier to seek out Klimt masterpieces in the Leopold Museum and quirky gifts in quartier21. Nip over to Spittelberg for an alfresco lunch on the cobblestones. Pause by the roses in the Volksgarten, then get your cultural fix with Rembrandt and Warhol originals in the splendid Albertina.

2–3 DAYS: SHORT CITY-BREAK

Follow in Strauss' footsteps by composing your own waltz at the House of Music, see Lipizzaner stallions perform at the Spanish Riding School and head to Leopoldstadt to stand in awe of Hundertwasser's crazed colours and contours. By night try *Wiener Schnitzel* and fruity Rieslings at vaulted wine cellar Esterházykeller, and enjoy theatrical highs at the illuminated Burgtheater. Go clubbing till dawn in the Volksgarten overlooking the palace.

Rent a bike to cycle trails weaving through the Prater (stopping for a ride on the iconic Ferris wheel). In summer, cool off with a dip in one of the lidos on the banks of the Danube Canal. Before you return, pick up gifts from the high-street stores lining Mariahilfer Strasse.

LONGER: ENJOYING VIENNA TO THE FULL

If time isn't a problem, stay longer to discover the region's rich pickings. Go west to the Wienerwald to see Seegrotte Hinterbrühl (Europe's largest subterranean lake), glimpse precipitous gorges and hill walk in tranquil nature reserves. Take the thermal waters in Baden and climb Leopold-Figl-Warte for far-reaching alpine views.

An hour's drive from Vienna, the River Danube snakes through the Wachau Valley. This UNESCO World Heritage Site has a clutch of Benedictine abbeys, clifftop castles and gently sloping vineyards.

🔺 *Sacher: the ultimate Viennese coffee house*

Something for nothing

If you're on a tight budget, you'll be pleased to know that plenty of Vienna's sights can be enjoyed for free. Kick off your stay with a poke through the biggest and most vibrant food market, the Naschmarkt, to immerse yourself in local flavour. Swap the grand concert halls for street entertainment in the shadow of St Stephen's Cathedral, where first-rate puppeteers, musicians and opera singers give the pros a run for their money.

For the cost of a tram ticket, you can arrange your personalised tour of the sights on the Ring – take U-Bahn

◆ *Chilling out in the Prater costs nothing*

line 1 or 2 for fleeting glimpses of the immense Hofburg and neo-Gothic City Hall. Pause at the Volksgarten's attractive gardens strewn with fountains, flowers and sculptures. Stepping over to Landstrasse, art lovers gawp at the Hundertwasserhaus, an explosion of colour and mosaics that doesn't cost a penny to admire.

You can easily spend an afternoon combing the hip Spittelberg district's warren of cobbled streets, punctuated with beautiful Biedermeier townhouses, art studios and pavement cafés.

Nature costs nothing in the University of Vienna Botanical Gardens, where you can spot alpine species, tropical ferns and Antarctic beech trees. Join the locals to stroll through the shady Prater on a Sunday morning and pop into the dinky Museum for the Art of Entertainment for a free taste of circus life. On the city's fringes, visit the Lainzer Tiergarten with its peaceful oak woods where you can spy red deer, wild boar and woodpeckers.

In summer, the Danube Island is at the heart of the action. Locals come here to walk, swim, cycle, canoe or simply chill out on the stretch of beach they call Copa Cagrana.

FREE FESTIVALS

Spring and summer step up a gear with a host of free festivals. The pick of the bunch are the City Festival (April) with theatre, concerts and late-night parties, the cultural highs of the Vienna Festival (May–June) and the open-air concerts at the Danube Island Festival (June).

When it rains

With more indoor sights, museums and shops than you can shake a stick at, there's no need to let sudden downpours put a dampener on your stay in Vienna. Head for the city's shopping malls and galleries, snuggle up in a *Heurige* wine cellar to taste local tipples, or warm up Viennese-style in one of the gorgeous coffee houses.

Serving delicious pastries, free newspapers and a dollop of culture, the capital's cafés help you forget the wet weather. Sip a frothy mocha beneath vaulted ceilings in elegant Central, browse magazines in wood-panelled Sperl, or visit the celebrated Sacher for a slice of rich chocolaty *Sachertorte*.

When the heavens open, the locals love to shop. Join them in the central Steffl department store and the smart Ringstrassen

● *While away a rainy day at Schönbrunn Palace*

Galerien mall. A relative newcomer to the indoor shopping scene is Simmering's sprawling Gasometer. This revamped, red-bricked gas holder houses a futuristic mall with 70 shops, an entertainment centre and multiplex cinema.
Ⓦ www.gasometer.org

The city's galleries are an obvious choice when rain sets in. Take shelter in the Belvedere, which has everything from Klimt paintings to medieval masterpieces, or go to the KunstHaus Wien, with its wonderful Hundertwasser works hung on wonky walls. And don't forget the MuseumsQuartier, with attractions including Architecturzentrum Wien, the Kunsthalle Wien, the Leopold Museum, MUMOK and the ZOOM Kindermuseum.

SCHÖNBRUNN PALACE

Allow a day to take in this magnificent UNESCO World Heritage Site, once Sisi's baroque summer residence. It's one of the most important cultural monuments in Austria, with its palace, park and zoo (see page 132) visited by some 6.7 million people a year. Feel the heat of the tropics in the 20-m (66-ft) high Palm House and view the Hall of Mirrors where Mozart once played. The Imperial Coach Collection gleams with golden carriages and the Millions Room has magnificent rosewood panelling. There are tours around the Imperial apartments. ⓐ Schönbrunner Schlossstrasse ⓣ 01 811 130 Ⓦ www.schoenbrunn.at ⓑ 08.30–16.30 Mon–Sun (winter); 08.30–18.00 (summer) Ⓜ U-Bahn: U4 Schönbrunn. Admission charge

On arrival

TIME DIFFERENCES
Like the rest of Austria, Vienna runs on Central European Time (CET), an hour ahead of Greenwich Mean Time (GMT) and two hours ahead during daylight savings. In the Austrian summer, at 12.00 noon, time at home is as follows:

Australia: Eastern Standard Time 20.00, Central Standard Time 19.30, Western Standard Time 18.00
New Zealand: 22.00
South Africa: 12.00
UK: 11.00
USA: Eastern Time 06.00, Central Time 05.00, Mountain Time 04.00, Pacific Time 03.00, Alaska 02.00.

ARRIVING
By air
Situated 20 km (12 miles) from the centre, Vienna International Airport serves European destinations including London, Paris and Berlin. No-frills airlines offering cheap flights include Germanwings and Air Berlin. The user-friendly airport has services including ATMs, shops, currency exchange and cafés. Departing every 30 minutes from 06.00 to 23.00, the City Airport Train whisks you to central Vienna (Landstrasse/Wien Mitte) in 16 minutes (about €15 return). A taxi into town costs around €30. ❶ 01 7007 Ⓦ www.viennaairport.com

A budget alternative is to travel with Ryanair from London Stansted or Dublin to Bratislava in Slovakia, 60 km (36 miles) from Vienna. ⓦ www.airportbratislava.sk

By rail

If you travel by train to Vienna, you'll arrive at Südbahnhof or Westbahnhof. Austria's national rail network ÖBB runs an efficient service to major cities including Salzburg, Innsbruck and Linz, plus international destinations like Berlin, Paris, Munich, Basel and Bratislava. Both stations offer left luggage facilities, toilets, newsagents and cafés.
ⓦ www.oebb.at

By bus

Most international and long-distance buses pull into central bus stations including Landstrasse/Wien Mitte, Südbahnhof and Schwedenplatz. Eurolines and National Express operate a frequent service. ☏ 01 711 01 (bus information)

By car

Vienna is well connected to the rest of Austria and Europe via the A1, A2 and A4 Autobahns. To drive on Austria's motorways, it's a legal requirement that you display a *Vignette* (toll sticker) in the front windscreen, which you can buy at the airport or in petrol stations. Short-stay parking is available in central Vienna (districts 1 to 9 and 20) – you'll need a valid *Parkschein* (parking ticket) which you can buy from most newsagents. Some hotels can arrange an all-day parking permit.

FINDING YOUR FEET

Vienna is generally a safe city and the crime rate is low. It's unlikely you'll experience any problems during your stay, but it's wise to exert caution if walking in dimly lit, less-populated areas at night. Pickpockets sometimes target travellers in crowded areas of the city, so be aware of where you have your handbag or wallet.

ORIENTATION

The city splits into 23 districts (*Bezirke*), each with its own flavour and attractions. Many sights including the Hofburg and St Stephen's Cathedral cluster in the historic centre (*Innere Stadt*) encircled by the 4-km (2.5-mile) Ringstrasse, a wide boulevard often simply called the Ring. Districts 1 to 9 represent the city centre (*Innenbezirke*) and spider out to Vienna's outer districts (*Außenbezirke*).

Heading west you reach the MuseumsQuartier in Neubau, while Leopoldstadt and Landstrasse to the east are home to the Hundertwasserhaus and Prater Park's enormous Ferris wheel. Schönbrunn Palace (see page 49) is situated 4.5 km (3 miles) south of the centre in Hietzing.

GETTING AROUND

An efficient public transport network makes getting around easy. If you're planning on making more than one trip, save by buying a 24-hour pass for about €5 or a 72-hour network pass for about €17, which offers unlimited use of the city's trams, buses and U-Bahn (metro). Remember to stamp your ticket the first time you travel. Wiener Linien provides detailed maps and timetables. ⓦ www.wienerlinien.at

By metro

Operating from 06.00 to 24.00 daily, the speedy U-Bahn system features five lines that criss-cross the city and travel to the suburbs: U1, U2, U3, U4 and U6 (there is no U5).

By tram

Vienna's red-and-white trams are a scenic way of getting about town. Trams run every five to ten minutes from 06.00 to 24.00 and you'll find timetables at every stop.

By bus

Around 80 bus lines streak the city and night buses operate along the main routes every 30 minutes until 05.00. Sightseeing buses offer guided tours where you can hop on and off as you please. Ⓦ www.viennasightseeing.at

○ *Trams are a speedy way to get around the Ring*

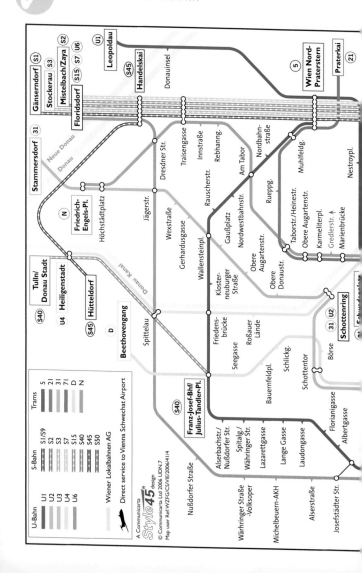

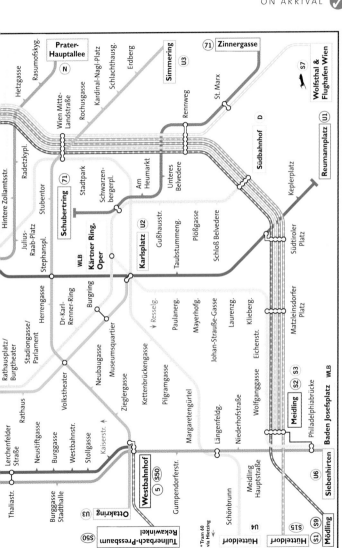

By taxi

Taxis operate on a meter (there's a surcharge for luggage and trips after 23.00), but negotiate the fare first if you want to travel to the city's suburbs. Tip around 10 per cent of the fare.

CAR HIRE

There's no need to hire a car if you are exploring central Vienna's sights, as the city's excellent public transport network is a quicker, cheaper and more practical way of getting around. However, a car is recommended for discovering off-the-beaten-track parts of the Wienerwald and Wachau Valley.

IF YOU GET LOST, TRY ...

Excuse me, do you speak English?
Entschuldigen Sie, sprechen Sie Englisch?
Entshuldigen zee, shprekhen zee english?

Excuse me, is this the right way to the old town/the city centre/the tourist office/the station/the bus station?
Entschuldigung, geht es hier zur Altstadt/zur Stadtmitte/zur Touristeninformation/zum Bahnhof/zum Busbahnhof?
Entshuldeegoong, gayt es here tsoor altshtat/tsoor shtatmitter/zur touristeninformation/tsoom baanhof/tsoom busbaanhof?

Can you point to it on my map?
Können Sie es mir bitte auf der Karte zeigen?
Kernen see es meer bitter owf der kaarte tsygen?

⊙ *The impressive Parliament building can be seen from the Ring*

The city centre

Vienna's 1st district, a UNESCO World Heritage Site, is filled with awe-inspiring Habsburg palaces and resplendent cafés, acres of galleries and hip bars lining the Bermuda Triangle. First-timers to the Austrian capital often kick off their stay in the vibrant and walkable centre, with plenty to keep culture buffs, shopaholics and clubbers on their toes for days. Whiffs of strong coffee, the clip-clop of horse-drawn carriages and twinkling crown jewels – think Vienna at its picture-book best. Discover everything from puppeteers performing in the shadow of St Stephen's Cathedral to the joys of dancing beneath the stars at the Volksgarten.

SIGHTS & ATTRACTIONS

Hofburg (Imperial Palace)

For 600 years the epicentre of the Habsburg Empire, this immense palace complex is overwhelming. You could literally spend days roaming the lavish Imperial Apartments once inhabited by Emperor Franz Joseph I and Empress Elisabeth and still festooned with Bohemian crystal chandeliers and Biedermeier portraits. Other highlights include the Sisi Museum, Silver Collection and Imperial Court Chapel where the celebrated Vienna Boys' Choir sings every Sunday.
ⓐ Kaisertor/Innerer Burghof ⓣ 01 533 7570
ⓦ www.hofburg-wien.at ⓔ info@hofburg-wien.at
ⓛ 09.00–17.00 Mon–Sun ⓥ U-Bahn: U3 Herrengasse.
Admission charge

Rathaus (Vienna City Hall)

Rising high above the square, Vienna's neo-Gothic City Hall strikes you with its slender 98-m (322-ft) tower and *Eiserner Rathausmann* (Iron Knight). It looks impressive lit up by night.
🅰 Rathausplatz 🕿 01 525 50 🕒 Guided tours 13.00 Mon, Wed & Fri Ⓜ U-Bahn: U2 Rathaus

Ringstrasse (The Ring)

Vienna's city centre is encircled by the Ringstrasse, a boulevard built on the old city walls that's often simply called the Ring.

🔺 *Hofburg Palace*

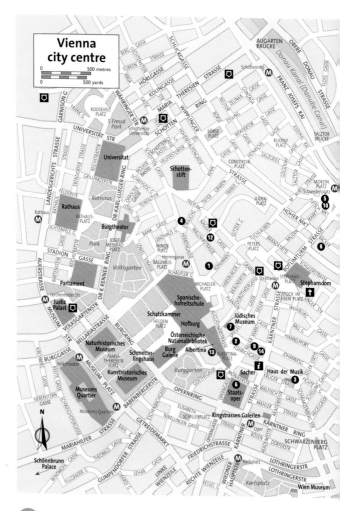

Vienna
city centre

0   500 metres
0   500 yards

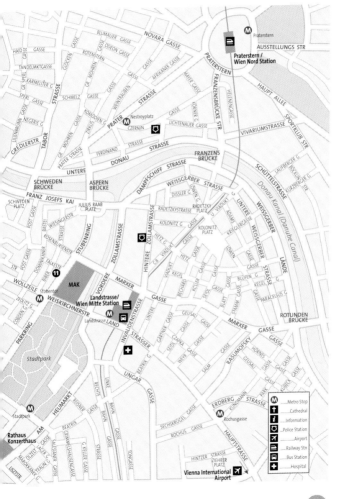

Hop on tram 1 or 2 to see the main sights, which include the Hofburg, the University of Vienna and Otto Wagner's Post Office Savings Bank.

ⓦ www.wien.info

Spanischehofreitschule (Spanish Riding School)

See the Lipizzaner stallions in action at the Hofburg's school for classical riding. Enjoy the morning exercises to music or one of the full performances.

ⓐ Michaelerplatz 1 ⓣ 01 533 9031 ⓦ www.srs.at ⓔ office@srs.at ⓛ Morning exercises 10.00–12.00 Tues–Sat; performances 11.00 Sun ⓝ U-Bahn: U3 Herrengasse. Admission charge

Stephansdom (St Stephen's Cathedral)

Soaring above Stephansplatz square, this Gothic cathedral is one of Vienna's most iconic landmarks with its skeletal spires and zigzag mosaic-tiled roof (see photo, page 75). The tower, at 137 m (448 ft), was completed in 1433 and was for many years

---

WINGED BEAUTIES

Set in the beautiful Burggarten, the Art Nouveau Schmetterlingshaus (Butterfly House) is alive with tiny wings. Glance up to see more than 400 butterflies fluttering past tropical foliage. You can even get married here. ⓐ Burggarten ⓣ 01 533 8570 ⓦ www.schmetterlingshaus.at ⓛ 10.00–16.45 Mon–Fri, 10.00–18.15 Sat–Sun (Apr–Oct); 10.00–15.45 Mon–Sun (Nov–Mar) ⓝ U-Bahn: U1 Karlsplatz. Admission charge

the tallest building in Europe. Climb its 343 steps for far-reaching views over the rooftops. The cathedral's famous bell, the Pummerin, is used to ring in the New Year across the city.

ⓐ 1 Stephansplatz ⓣ 01 513 7648 ⓦ www.stephansdom.at ⓔ office@stephansdom.at ⓛ Guided tours 10.30 & 15.00 Mon–Sat, 15.00 Sun ⓝ U-Bahn: U1 Stephansplatz. Admission charge ⓘ At the time of writing the view from the South Tower was restricted due to renovations.

Volksgarten (People's Park)

Criss-crossed with paths and speckled with sculptures and fountains, this central pocket of greenery is a breath of fresh air. Stroll the rose gardens, spot the neoclassical Temple of Theseus and marble monument to Empress Elisabeth, then pause for coffee and cake in the octagonal pavilion.

ⓐ Burgring ⓝ U-Bahn: U3 Volkstheater

CULTURE

Albertina

Art buffs are in their element at this grand Habsburg palace, which houses a stunning collection of prints and drawings. The Graphic Collection displays works by Rembrandt and Rubens, plus 20th-century Warhol and Picasso works. Under the same roof are the Photographic Collection, Architecture Collection and Poster Collection.

ⓐ Albertinaplatz 1 ⓣ 01 534 830 ⓦ www.albertina.at ⓔ info@albertina.at ⓛ 10.00–18.00 Thur–Tues, 10.00–21.00 Wed ⓝ U-Bahn: U1 Karlsplatz. Admission charge

Burgtheater (National Theatre)

Opened in 1888, this former imperial court theatre stages world-class opera and contemporary and classic plays. The repertoire and opulent interior are impressive.

ⓐ Dr-Karl-Lueger-Ring 2 ⓣ 01 51444/4140 ⓦ www.burgtheater.at
ⓔ info@burgtheater.at ⓛ Sept–June; closed Jul–Aug
Ⓝ U-Bahn: U2 Rathaus

Haus der Musik (House of Music)

Get loud at this state-of-the-art museum with larger-than-life instruments. Compose your own waltz with the Waltz Dice game, create a CD in the Evolution Machine or conduct the Vienna Philharmonic (virtually, of course!).

ⓐ Seilerstätte 30 ⓦ www.hausdermusik.com ⓣ 01 516 48
ⓔ info@hdm.at ⓛ 10.00–22.00 Mon–Sun Ⓝ U-Bahn: U1
Karlsplatz. Admission charge

Jüdisches Museum (Jewish Museum)

Set in a historic mansion, this thought-provoking museum has a permanent exhibition on medieval Jewry and showcases the excavations of a medieval synagogue.

ⓐ Judenplatz 8 ⓣ 01 535 0431 ⓦ www.jmw.at ⓛ 10.00–18.00
Sun–Fri; closed Sat Ⓝ U-Bahn: U1 Stephansplatz.
Admission charge

Kunsthistorisches Museum (Art History Museum)

Feast your eyes on yet more of the House of Habsburg's art treasures. The domed Renaissance-style museum houses a wonderful collection. The walls of the Picture Gallery are hung with works by Rubens, Caravaggio and Titian, and there are supplementary collections including Egyptian antiquities and Roman pottery.

ⓐ Maria-Theresien-Platz ⓣ 01 525 240 ⓕ 01 525 24 503
ⓦ www.khm.at ⓔ info@khm.at ⓛ 10.00–18.00 Tues–Sun, closed Mon ⓝ U-Bahn: U3 Volkstheater. Admission charge

MAK (Museum of Applied Arts)

MAK's rich collection stretches from Wiener Werkstätte pieces, art deco friezes, medieval silk embroideries and Persian carpets right up to architectural models by Frank Gehry.

ⓐ Stubenring 5 ⓣ 01 711 360 ⓦ www.mak.at ⓔ office@mak.at
ⓛ 10.00–12.00 Tues, 10.00–18.00 Wed–Sun, closed Mon
ⓝ U-Bahn: U3 Stubentor. Admission charge

Österreichische Nationalbibliothek (Austrian National Library)

Gaze up at the State Hall's frescoes in Europe's largest baroque library, which houses a Globe Museum and Papyrus Museum tracing life in Ancient Egypt, a collection of writings by Martin Luther, and thousands of priceless books.

ⓐ Josefsplatz 1 ⓣ 01 534 10 ⓦ www.onb.ac.at ⓔ onb@onb.ac.at
ⓛ 10.00–18.00 Tues–Sun, 10.00–21.00, closed Mon ⓝ U-Bahn: U1 Stephansplatz. Admission charge

Schatzkammer (Imperial Treasury)

Glittering with jewel-encrusted orbs, vestments and crowns, the wealth of the Hofburg treasury is truly mind-boggling. Take a peek at the Holy Roman Empire jewels.

ⓐ Schweizerhof ⓣ 01 525 240 ⓦ www.khm.at ⓔ info.kk@khm.at

🕐 10.00–18.00 Wed–Mon, closed Tue 🔵 U-Bahn: U1
Stephansplatz. Admission charge

Staatsoper (Vienna State Opera)

Vienna's 19th-century opera house is one of the world's
greatest. As well as performances by the acclaimed
Philharmonic Orchestra, the venue stages first-rate opera
and ballet and special performances for children.

🔺 *The Mozart statue in the Burggarten*

ⓐ Opernring 2 **ⓣ** 01 513 1 513 **ⓦ** www.wiener-staatsoper.at
ⓔ information@wiener-staatsoper.at **ⓝ** U-Bahn: U1 Karlsplatz

RETAIL THERAPY

Altmann & Kühne The handmade bonbons and pralines here
are confection perfection. **ⓐ** Am Graben 30 **ⓣ** 01 533 0927
ⓦ www.feinspitz.com **ⓛ** 09.00–18.30 Mon–Fri, 10.00–17.00 Sat,
closed Sun **ⓝ** U-Bahn: U1 Stephansplatz

Bernhardt Clubbers kit themselves out with Diesel and Miss
Sixty styles here. **ⓐ** Kärntner Strasse 35 **ⓣ** 01 512 9103
ⓛ 10.00–19.00 Mon–Fri, 10.00–17.00 Sat, closed Sun **ⓝ** U-Bahn:
U1 Stephansplatz

Boehle Hundreds of Austrian and international wines share
shelf space with pâtés and preserves. **ⓐ** Wollzeile 30 **ⓣ** 01 512
3155 **ⓦ** www.boehle.at **ⓛ** 08.30–19.00 Mon–Fri, 08.30–17.00 Sat,
closed Sun **ⓝ** U-Bahn: U1 Stephansplatz

Demmers Teehaus Unusual teas like meditation, Greek
mountain and alpine bloom blends are in plentiful supply here.
ⓐ Mölkerbastei 5 **ⓣ** 01 533 5995 **ⓦ** www.demmer.at
ⓛ 09.30–18.00 Mon–Fri, 09.30–12.30 Sat, closed Sun **ⓝ** U-Bahn:
U1 Stephansplatz

Meinl am Graben Foodies sniff out specialities like Wachau
apricot jam, Mozartkugeln pralines and Spanish *pata negra* ham
here. **ⓐ** Graben 19 **ⓣ** 01 532 3334 **ⓦ** www.meinlamgraben.at

🕐 08.30–19.30 Mon–Wed, 08.30–20.00 Thur–Fri, 09.00–18.00 Sat, closed Sun 🚇 U-Bahn: U1 Stephansplatz

Österreichische Werkstätten Quality Austrian handicrafts from glassware to jewellery fill this store. Dig deep – it's not cheap!
🅰 Kärntner Strasse 6 ☎ 01 512 2418 🌐 www.austrianarts.at
🕐 07.00–20.00 Mon–Sun 🚇 U-Bahn: U1 Stephansplatz

Ringstrassen Galerien This smart mall is the place to buy Aigner shoes and Swarovski crystals. There's also a florist, perfumery, juice and sushi bar. 🅰 Kärntner Ring 5–7 ☎ 01 512 5181
🌐 www.ringstrassen-galerien.at 🕐 10.00–19.00 Mon–Fri, 10.00–18.00 Sat, closed Sun 🚇 U-Bahn: U1 Stephansplatz

Steffl From MAC cosmetics to designer gear by Armani and Esprit, this sleek department store houses 50 shops under one roof. 🅰 Kärntner Strasse 19 ☎ 01 514 310 🌐 www.kaufhaus-steffl.at 🕐 09.30–19.00 Mon–Fri, 09.30–18.00 Sat, closed Sun
🚇 U-Bahn: U1 Stephansplatz

TAKING A BREAK

Café Demel £ ❶ Indulge in pastries or dainty sandwiches with coffee in the beautifully preserved rococo salon and pick up a bag of the famous candied violets before you leave.
🅰 Kohlmarkt 14 ☎ 01 535 17170 🌐 www.demel.at 🕐 10.00–19.00 Mon–Sun 🚇 U-Bahn: U3 Herrengasse

Café Tirolerhof £ ❷   Opposite the Albertina, this traditional
Viennese café whips up strong coffee and a mean apple strudel.
ⓐ Führichgasse 8 ⓣ 01 512 7833 ⓛ 07.00–22.00 Mon–Sat,
09.00–20.00 Sun ⓝ U-Bahn: U1 Karlsplatz

Cantino £ ❸   On the top floor of the House of Music, this
restaurant overlooking St Stephen's offers value-for-money
lunches including ricotta ravioli and pumpkin risotto.
ⓐ Seilerstätte 30 ⓣ 01 512 5446 ⓦ www.cantino.at
ⓛ 12.00–15.00, 18.00–23.00 Mon–Sat, 12.00–15.00 Sun
ⓝ U-Bahn: U4 Stadtpark

Central £ ❹   Hear the piano tinkle and devour delicious
pastries at this literary café, where vaulted ceilings and columns
add a dash of old-world grandeur. ⓐ Herrengasse/Strauchgasse
ⓣ 01 533 37 64 24 ⓦ www.palaisevents.at ⓛ 07.30–22.00
Mon–Sat, 10.00–18.00 Sun ⓝ U-Bahn: U1 Karlsplatz

Maschu Maschu £ ❺   This dinky restaurant promises the best
falafel in town – it delivers! ⓐ Rabensteig 8 ⓣ 01 533 2904
ⓦ www.maschu-maschu.at ⓛ 11.30–24.00 Sun–Wed,
11.30–04.00 Thur–Sat ⓝ U-Bahn: U1 Schwedenplatz

Sacher £ ❻   If you want to try the mother of all *Sachertorte*
chocolate cakes (baked according to the original 1832 recipe),
head for this quintessential Viennese café.
ⓐ Philharmonikerstrasse 4 ⓣ 01 51 4560 ⓦ www.sacher.com
ⓛ 08.00–24.00 Mon–Sun ⓝ U-Bahn: U1 Karlsplatz

Trzesniewski £ ❼ Little gem of a café, with some of Vienna's best open sandwiches. Try them with a *Pfiff* – the tiniest beer you've ever seen. ⓐ Dorotheergasse 1 ⓣ 01 512 3291 ⓦ www.trzesniewski.at ⓛ 08.30–19.30 Mon–Fri, 09.00–17.00 Sat, closed Sun ⓝ U-Bahn: U1 Stephansplatz

Zanoni & Zanoni £ ❽ Refresh with *gelati*, a prosciutto panini or espresso on the terrace of this excellent Italian ice-cream parlour. ⓐ Lugeck 7 ⓣ 01 512 7979 ⓦ www.zanoni.co.at ⓛ 07.00–24.00 Mon–Sun ⓝ U-Bahn: U1 Stephansplatz

AFTER DARK

Restaurants
Barbaro Bistro £ ❾ This avant-garde bistro and wine bar has wood-fired pizza and yummy finger food. ⓐ Neuer Markt 8 ⓣ 01 955 2525 ⓦ www.barbaro.at ⓔ barbaro@barbaro.at ⓛ 08.00–04.00 Mon–Sun ⓝ U-Bahn: U1 Stephansplatz

Bermuda Brennerei £ ❿ Tuck into Austrian favourites like schnitzel and goulash, washed down with homebrews, in this lively gastro pub. ⓐ Rabensteig 6 ⓣ 01 532 2865 ⓦ www.bermuda-braeu.at ⓛ 11.00–04.00 Mon–Sat, 11.00–02.00 Sun ⓝ U-Bahn: U1 Schwedenplatz

Castillo Comida £ ⓫ Spice up your evening with Caribbean specialities like jerk chicken, goat curry and chilli-fuelled 'pepper pot' made to make your eyes water. Sip mojitos or daiquiris at the rum bar. ⓐ Stubenring 20 ⓣ 01 512 9404

ⓦ www.castillo-comida.at ⓔ castillo@aon.at ⓛ 11.00–15.00
Mon–Fri, 18.00–01.00 Mon–Sat ⓝ U-Bahn: U3 Stubenring

Esterházykeller £ ⓬ Go underground to this vaulted
17th-century *Heurige* (wine cellar) with exposed brickwork,
wood panelling and an impressive wine list. Hearty fare includes
pork roast, dumplings and strudel. ⓐ Haarhof 1 ⓣ 01 533 3482
ⓦ www.esterhazykeller.at ⓛ 11.00–23.00 Mon–Fri, 16.00–23.00
Sat–Sun ⓝ U-Bahn: U3 Herrengasse

Palmenhaus ££ ⓭ Dine beneath palms and vines at the
art nouveau Palmenhaus, a glorious glass-fronted conservatory
with views over the Burggarten and Hofburg palace.
ⓐ Burggarten ⓣ 01 533 1033 ⓦ www.palmenhaus.at
ⓔ office@palmenhaus.at ⓛ 10.00–02.00 Mon–Sun (Mar–Oct);
10.00–02.00 Wed–Sun, closed Mon–Tue (Nov–Feb)
ⓝ U-Bahn: U1 Karlsplatz

Sky Bar £££ ⓮ Going up... Spy St Stephen's Cathedral from
the seventh-floor Sky Bar. All floor-to-ceiling glass, this place
isn't cheap, but the cuisine is gourmet and views priceless.
ⓐ Kärntner Strasse 19 ⓣ 01 513 1712 ⓦ www.skybar.at
ⓔ office@skybox.at ⓛ 18.00–01.00 Mon–Sat, closed Sun
ⓝ U-Bahn: U1 Stephansplatz

Bars & clubs
Club Habana Get your Latino groove on and sway all night long
to salsa, bachata and merengue. ⓐ Mahlerstrasse 11 ⓣ 01 513
2075 ⓦ www.clubhabana.at ⓔ people@clubhabana.at

🕒 19.30–04.00 Sun–Wed, 19.30–06.00 Thur–Sat Ⓝ U-Bahn: U1 Karlsplatz

Flex Bass-loaded club beside the Danube Canal with live acts and DJs spinning techno and drum and bass beats. ⓐ Donaukanal 1 ⓣ 01 533 7525 ⓦ www.flex.at ⓔ office@flex.at 🕒 20.00–04.00 Mon–Sun Ⓝ U-Bahn: U2 Schottenring

Jazzland This cellar bar has been jazzing up Vienna's after-dark scene since 1972, with live music every night. ⓐ Franz Josefs Kai 29 ⓣ 01 533 2575 ⓦ www.jazzland.at ⓔ office@jazzland.at 🕒 19.00–open end Mon–Sat, closed Sun Ⓝ U-Bahn: U1 Schwedenplatz

Krah Krah Laid-back pub serving 50 different kinds of beer. ⓐ Rabensteig 8 ⓣ 01 533 8193 ⓦ www.krah-krah.at 🕒 11.00–02.00 Mon–Sun Ⓝ U-Bahn: U1 Schwedenplatz

Red Room The walls at this trendy basement bar are so red they'd make a pillar box blush! DJs playing RnB and soul keep the dance floor full. ⓐ Stubenring 20 ⓣ 01 512 4024 🕒 20.00–open end Mon–Sat, closed Sun Ⓝ U-Bahn: U3 Stubenring

Volksgarten Vienna's beautiful people sip cocktails at this cool club overlooking gardens, which has an open-air ballroom in summer. ⓐ Burgring ⓣ 01 532 4241 ⓦ www.volksgarten.at 🕒 20.00–04.00 Mon–Sun Ⓝ U-Bahn: U2 Volkstheater

⬤ *The Sky Bar (page 73) has great views of St Stephen's Cathedral*

Neubau

So you've done your Habsburg palace bit, now head over to the 7th district to see what they've done to the imperial stables. They've turned into the MuseumsQuartier – one of the ten biggest cultural complexes in the world. The haunt of artists, dreamers and individualists, this district is beautifully compact and wonderfully quirky.

SIGHTS & ATTRACTIONS

quartier21

A vast space given over to independent cultural initiatives, contemporary arts and idiosyncratic shops, and with a thriving artist-in-residence scheme, quartier21 has plenty of surprises tucked up its sleeve. Rock down to Electric Avenue's galleries and boutiques, or discover the illuminated Tonspur passage, Play FM and Puls TV, Vienna's first local TV station.

ⓐ Museumsplatz 1 ⓦ http://quartier21.mqw.at
Ⓝ U-Bahn: U2 Museumsquartier

Spittelberg

Explore the Spittelberg's maze of narrow cobbled streets for a taste of old Vienna with a modern twist. Recently given a new lease of life, this has become one of the city's hippest enclaves, with a string of grand 18th-century Biedermeier houses, open-air cafés, hole-in-the-wall pubs, dinky art galleries and vibrant bars.

ⓦ www.spittelberg.at Ⓝ U-Bahn: U3 Volkstheater

⬤ *quartier21 is a cultural hotspot*

Neubau

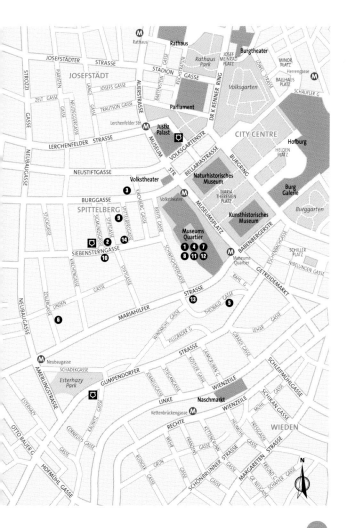

CULTURE

Architekturzentrum Wien

If you're into architecture, make time to visit this shrine to futuristic design. White walls, arches and sleek staircases set the scene for changing exhibitions, talks and workshops. Look out for the F3 Hall's vaulting, the octagonal library's skylight and the Old Hall's exposed brickwork.

ⓐ Museumsplatz 1 ⓣ 01 522 3115 ⓦ www.azw.at ⓔ office@azw.at ⓛ 10.00–19.00 Thur–Tues, 10.00–21.00 Wed ⓝ U-Bahn: U2 Museumsquartier. Admission charge

Dschungel Wien

Challenging conventions, this theatre aims its unique productions and workshops at young audiences. Alongside puppetry, dance and theatre, new media and experimental works play a big part.

ⓐ Museumsplatz 1 ⓣ 01 522 0720 ⓦ www.dschungelwien.at ⓔ office@dschungelwien.at ⓝ U-Bahn: U2 Museumsquartier

Halle E & G

Perched on the site of the former court stables and fusing baroque with modern architecture, this art space is a real audience grabber, hosting pioneering theatre, dance, music and opera, and the annual ImPulsTanz dance festival.

ⓐ Museumsplatz 1 ⓣ 01 524 33 210 ⓦ www.halleneg.at ⓛ 10.00–19.00 Thur–Tues, 10.00–21.00 Wed ⓝ U-Bahn: U2 Museumsquartier

Kunsthalle Wien

Enjoy experimental art in its different guises at this innovative museum. The 18th-century cream-coloured edifice has been revamped as a multimedia forum for contemporary paintings, photography, film and new media.

ⓐ Museumsplatz 1 ⓣ 01 52189 1201 ⓦ www.kunsthallewien.at ⓛ 10.00–22.00 Thur, 10.00–19.00 Fri–Wed ⓝ U-Bahn: U2 Museumsquartier. Admission charge

Leopold Museum

Set in a vast white limestone cube, the museum houses Rudolf Leopold's formerly private collection. The light-flooded galleries showcase 19th- and 20th-century masterpieces on five levels, including important works by Gustav Klimt, Oskar Kokoschka, Egon Schiele and Herbert Boeckl. Klimt's mosaic-like *Tod und Leben* (Death and Life) raises eyebrows.

ⓐ Museumsplatz 1 ⓣ 01 525 700 ⓦ www.leopoldmuseum.org ⓛ 10.00–18.00 Wed–Mon, 10.00–21.00 Thur, closed Tues ⓝ U-Bahn: U2 Museumsquartier. Admission charge

MUMOK (Museum of Modern Art Ludwig Foundation)

Soaring above Museumsplatz square, this grey lava stone megalith houses Austria's largest contemporary art museum. Behind the sturdy bricks, you'll find a superb collection of 7,000 works spanning 20th-century movements including Pop Art, New Realism, Expressionism and Surrealism. Among the big names whose work graces the walls are Picasso, Magritte, Kandinsky and Klee. Look out for Andy Warhol's striking *Orange Car Crash*.

ⓐ Museumsplatz 1 ⓣ 01 525 00 ⓦ www.mumok.at

🕐 10.00–18.00 Tues–Sun, 10.00–21.00 Thurs, closed Mon
Ⓝ U-Bahn: U2 Museumsquartier. Admission charge

Tanzquartier Wien

Cutting-edge centre for contemporary choreographies, bringing the best of national and international dance to the MuseumsQuartier.
ⓐ Museumsplatz 1 ⓣ 01 581 3591 Ⓕ 01 581 3591 12
Ⓦ www.tqw.at Ⓝ U-Bahn: U2 Museumsquartier

Volkstheater (People's Theatre)

This turn-of-the-century theatre shows an eclectic mix of classics, new plays and avant-garde interpretations from Shakespeare to chanson. Sip drinks beneath the chandeliers in the frescoed Rote Bar before the performance.
ⓐ Neustiftgasse 1 ⓣ 01 521 110 Ⓦ www.volkstheater.at Ⓝ U-Bahn: U3 Volkstheater

ZOOM Kindermuseum

Kids can pull and prod in the Zoom Ozean, or create cartoons and record their own music in the Zoom Lab at Austria's only children's museum. Activities need to be pre-booked.
ⓐ Museumsplatz 1 ⓣ 01 524 7908 Ⓦ www.kindermuseum.at
Ⓝ U-Bahn: U2 Museumsquartier. Admission charge

RETAIL THERAPY

a1 Lounge This whiter-than-white store dazzles with the latest mobile phone technology and a luminous bar on the upper

level. ⓐ Mariahilfer Strasse 60 ⓣ 01 526 0026 ⓦ
www.a1lounge.at ⓛ 09.30–19.30 Mon–Fri, 09.00–18.00 Sat,
closed Sun ⓝ U-Bahn: U3 Neubaug

Be a Good Girl Divas with attitude pick up quirky shoes, shirts
and bags, slip into a new pair of Levi's and get their hair snipped
in the salon. ⓐ Westbahnstrasse 5a ⓣ 01 524 4728
ⓦ www.beagoodgirl.com ⓛ 10.00–18.00 Mon, 10.00–19.00
Tues–Fri, 10.00–17.00 Sat, closed Sun ⓝ Bus 13A: Zieglergasse

Filz Faktor Trendy textile store where everything is made from
felt, ranging from brightly coloured berets and bags to soft
slippers and scarves. ⓐ Neubaugasse 1 ⓣ 01 944 6655
ⓦ www.filzfaktor.at ⓛ 11.00–18.00 Mon–Wed, 11.00–20.00 Thur
& Fri, 11.00–17.00 Sat, closed Sun ⓝ U-Bahn: U3 Volkstheater

△ *Old meets new in MuseumsQuartier*

Milk & Honey Psychedelic boutique with colourful clothing and original gifts from holograms and acid jazz records to wacky lamps and spray-painted toasters. Zollergasse 16 01 923 9399 11.00–19.00 Mon–Fri, 10.00–17.00 Sat U-Bahn: U2 Museumsquartier

Peek & Cloppenburg Fashionistas flock to this department store giant, which stocks labels like Adidas, Armani, Betty Barclay, Burberry, Diesel and Miss Sixty. Mariahilfer Strasse 26–30 01 525 610 www.peekundcloppenburg.at 10.00–19.00 Mon–Wed, 10.00–20.00 Thur & Fri, 09.30–18.00 Sat U-Bahn: U3 Neubaug

Prachner Browse for books on art, photography, design and architecture in this vaulted baroque hall, which doubles as a platform for lectures, presentations and literary events. Museumsplatz 1 01 512 8588 www.prachner.at 10.00–19.00 Mon–Sun U-Bahn: U2 Museumsquartier

Subotron Game freaks seek out technical wizardry at this electronics store. Test out the latest PC games, gadgets and music before you buy. Museumsplatz 1 http://shop.subotron.com 13.00–18.00 Wed–Sun, closed Mon & Tue U-Bahn: U2 Museumsquartier

TAKING A BREAK

Café Leopold £ ❶ This ultra-modern café's huge windows and terrace afford prime views over the MuseumsQuartier. By night,

it becomes a hip bar with DJs on the decks and film screenings.
ⓐ Museumsplatz 1 ⓣ 01 523 6732 ⓦ www.cafe-leopold.at
ⓛ 10.00–02.00 Sun–Wed, 10.00–04.00 Thur–Sat ⓝ U-Bahn: U2
Museumsquartier

Centimeter £ ❷   Order sandwiches by the centimetre and beer
by the litre at this fun spot. ⓐ Stiftgasse 4 ⓣ 01 470 0606
ⓦ www.centimeter.at ⓛ 10.30–02.00 Mon–Fri, 11.00–02.00 Sat,
11.00–24.00 Sun ⓝ U-Bahn: U3 Volkstheater

Das Möbel £ ❸   A lunch spot and interior design gallery rolled
into one. You can buy the chair you sit on if you've got the spare
change. The airy café serves snacks like fresh salads, quiches,
sandwiches and pastries. Try the ginger-lemon tea with banana
cake. ⓐ Burggasse 10 ⓣ 01 524 9497 ⓦ www.dasmoebel.at
ⓛ 10.00–01.00 Mon–Sun ⓝ U-Bahn: U3 Volkstheater

MUMOK Café £ ❹   An arched ceiling, glass walls and
communal tables create a feeling of space at the gallery's open-
plan café. The value-for-money lunch menu features
Mediterranean-inspired dishes and kids' favourites. Relax here
with coffee by day and cocktails by night. ⓐ Museumsplatz 1
ⓣ 01 505 001 440 ⓛ 10.00–23.00 Tues–Sun, closed Mon
ⓝ U-Bahn: U2 Museumsquartier

Sperl Concert Café £ ❺   With its dark wood panelling and low
lighting, this 19th-century Viennese café is a popular haunt. Sip
a double mocha with a slice of chocolatey Sachertorte or poppy
strudel and read the selection of international newspapers.

There's live music on a Sunday afternoon. ⓐ Gumpendorfer
Strasse 6 ⓣ 01 586 4158 ⓦ www.cafesperl.at ⓛ 07.00–23.00
Mon–Sat, 11.00–20.00 Sun ⓝ U-Bahn: U2 Museumsquartier

St. Art £ ❻ Enjoy a chai latte with ginger and cardamom or
freshly pressed juices at this café-cum-gallery. The menu
stretches from tasty snacks to exhibitions and live music.
ⓐ Zollergasse 6 ⓣ 01 522 6626 ⓦ www.st-art.at
ⓔ st-art@chello.at ⓛ 07.00–23.00 Mon–Sat, 11.00–20.00 Sun
ⓝ U-Bahn: U2 Museumsquartier

Una £ ❼ Striking café with a vaulted, black-and-white tiled
ceiling. The oriental-inspired artwork makes this a great spot to
take a break and check out the moreish menu. ⓐ Museumsplatz 1
ⓣ 01 523 6566 ⓛ 09.00–24.00 Mon–Fri, 10.00–24.00 Sat,
10.00–18.00 Sun ⓝ U-Bahn: U2 Museumsquartier

Unter'm Hollerbusch £ ❽ Pause for organic coffee and snacks
to eat in or take away at this health-inspired shop near the main
entrance. ⓐ Museumsplatz 1 ⓣ 01 526 5303 ⓛ 09.00–19.00
Mon–Fri, 09.00–18.00 Sat, closed Sun ⓝ U-Bahn: U2
Museumsquartier

AFTER DARK

Restaurants
Amerlingbeisel £ ❾ Munch on tender lamb or tofu with
apple chutney beneath a canopy of trees in this relaxed
restaurant's inner courtyard. ⓐ Stiftgasse 8 ⓣ 01 526 1660

Ⓦ www.amerlingbeisl.at Ⓔ kontakt@amerlingbeisl.at
Ⓛ 09.00–02.00 Mon–Sat, closed Sun Ⓝ U-Bahn: U3
Volkstheater

Epos £ Ⓜ The design is simple but food delicious at this Middle
Eastern restaurant. Tuck into stuffed vine leaves, lamb and okra
stew and sticky baklava. Ⓐ Siebensterngasse 13/2 Ⓣ 01 526 0219
Ⓦ www.restaurantepos.at Ⓔ office@restaurantepos.at
Ⓛ 11.00–23.00 Mon–Sat, closed Sun Ⓝ U-Bahn: U3 Volkstheater

🔺 *MuseumsQuartier has rapidly developed its own identity*

Glacis Beisl £ ⓫ Pull up a chair on the tree-fringed terrace or in the conservatory for Viennese fare like beef goulash with pickles and Styrian kraut pasta. Quirky touches here include the aquarium and a 'growing picture' – a wall sprouting plants and flowers. ⓐ Museumsplatz 1 ⓣ 01 526 5660 ⓦ www.glacisbeisl.at ⓔ mail@glacisbeisl.at ⓛ 11.00–02.00 Mon–Sun ⓝ U-Bahn: U2 Museumsquartier

Halle £ ⓬ Cylindrical lights, arched windows and sheer drapes set the scene at this high-ceilinged restaurant, where you can dine on Italian flavours such as polenta with porcini mushrooms, or relax with drinks on the buzzy terrace. ⓐ Museumsplatz 1 ⓣ 01 523 7001 ⓦ www.diehalle.at ⓔ halle@motto.at ⓛ 10.00–02.00 Mon–Sun ⓝ U-Bahn: U2 Museumsquartier

Bar Italia ££ ⓭ One of the coolest places to dine in the 7th district, this Italian restaurant serves specialities like wild garlic ravioli and pumpkin gnocchi. Sip cocktails at the low-lit bar. ⓐ Mariahilfer Strasse 19–21 ⓣ 01 585 28 38 ⓦ www.baritalia.net ⓛ 18.30–02.00 Mon–Sat, closed Sun ⓝ U-Bahn: U3 Neubaug

Bohème ££ ⓮ Savour Austrian fusion cuisine at this snug restaurant with a cavernous wine cellar. Seafood lovers can sample dishes like Norwegian salmon and monkfish with a glass of crisp Grüner Veltliner. ⓐ Spittelberggasse 19 ⓣ 01 523 3173 ⓦ www.boheme.at ⓔ tisch@boheme.at ⓛ 11.00–24.00 Mon–Sun ⓝ U-Bahn: U3 Volkstheater

Bars & clubs

Blue Box Chilled café where the DJs spin everything from electro and techno beats to soul and ska. ⓐ Richtergasse 8 ⓣ 01 532 2682 ⓦ www.bluebox.at ⓛ 10.00–02.00 Tues–Sun, 18.00–02.00 Mon ⓝ U-Bahn: U3 Volkstheater

Europa Hinterzimmer Urbanites dance till the wee hours at this funky club where the DJs play jazz, hip hop, funk and drum'n'bass grooves. ⓐ Zollergasse 8 ⓣ 01 526 3383 ⓦ www.hinterzimmer.at ⓛ 22.00–04.00 Mon–Sun ⓝ U-Bahn: U3 Volkstheater

Kantine Sip cocktails at the onyx bar of this high-ceilinged bar decked out with oversized glitter balls and squishy sofas. ⓐ Museumsplatz 1 ⓣ 01 523 8239 ⓛ 10.00–24.00 Mon–Wed, 10.00–02.00 Thur–Sun ⓝ U-Bahn: U2 Museumsquartier

Siebenstern Bräu Drink homebrews beside copper kegs at this Spittelberg haunt. The adventurous can slurp fiery 7 Stern chilli beer or Bamberger Rauchbier smoked over beechwood. ⓐ Siebensterngasse 17 ⓣ 01 523 8697 ⓦ www.7stern.at ⓛ 10.00–24.00 Mon–Sun ⓝ U-Bahn: U3 Volkstheater

Stylez Spacey bar where trendies sip mint daiquiris and the walls glow red and gold. At Wednesday's Wellness Lounge, DJ Delani entertains and free massages make for good karma. ⓐ Neubaugasse 10 ⓣ 01 990 75 83 ⓦ www.stylez.at ⓛ 12.00–02.00 Mon–Sat, 12.00–24.00 Sun ⓝ U-Bahn: U3 Volkstheater

Leopoldstadt & Landstrasse

With the Prater's big wheel turning and Hundertwasser's crazy colours turning heads, Vienna's 2nd and 3rd districts are bound to put a spring in your step. By night, discover snug brewery pubs and clubs with urban edge.

Whether you want to drift along the Danube to drink in the city's sights or see masterpieces by Gustav Klimt at the Belvedere, this corner of Vienna mixes back-to-nature highs and cultural thrills. Avid shoppers should bring an oversized suitcase and make a beeline for the glut of high-street stores and chichi boutiques lining Landstrasser Hauptstrasse. By night, discover snug brewpubs with creaking beams and hip clubs with urban edge.

SIGHTS & ATTRACTIONS

Augarten

Once an imperial hunting lodge, this baroque palace overlooks a vast expanse of greenery – a great place for a stroll or picnic when the sun shines. Today the site houses Augarten Porcelain, where you can admire (or buy if you've got the spare change) some of Austria's finest handmade ceramics.

ⓐ Obere Augartenstrasse 1 ⓣ 01 211 2418 ⓦ www.augarten.at
ⓔ augarten@augarten.at ⓛ 09.30–17.00 Mon–Fri; closed Sat–Sun ⓝ Tram N: Radetzkyplatz

Danube boat trip

This round trip along the Danube Canal takes in key landmarks like the Prater and the lofty Danube Tower. The two-hour loop

aboard the MS *Vindobona* is a laid-back way to take in the sights.
🅰 Reichsbrücke 📞 01 588 80 585 🌐 www.donauschiff.at
🔵 U-Bahn: U1 Praterstern

Hundertwasserhaus
The ingenious Viennese architect Friedensreich Hundertwasser
went wild with his palette on this 50-apartment housing
complex. You can't fail to gawp at the explosion of colour and
irregular lines. Mirrored tiles, creeping vines and balconies
sprouting trees will have you reaching for your camera.
🅰 Löwengasse and Kegelgasse 📞 01 715 1553
🌐 www.hundertwasserhaus.at 🕐 Tour 13.45–15.15 Mon–Sun
🔵 Tram N: Radetzkyplatz

🔺 *Hundertwasserhaus is a sight to behold*

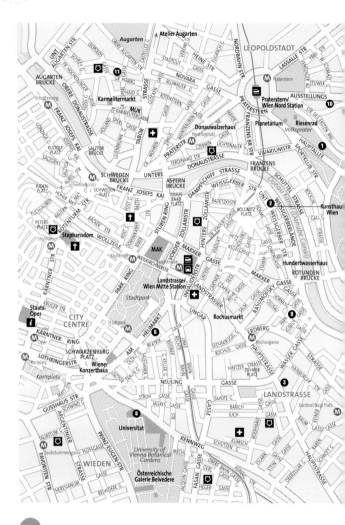

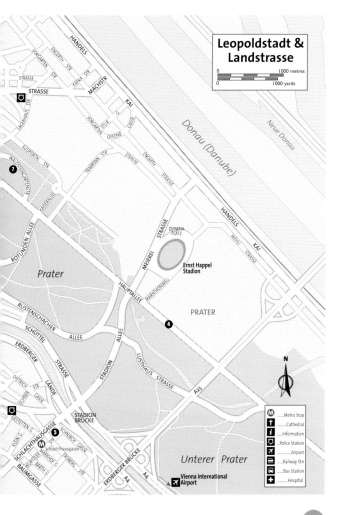

> **RAINBOW REBEL**
>
> The rebellious darling of Austrian art and architecture,
> Friedensreich Hundertwasser (1928–2000) believed
> that 'colourfulness, variety and diversity are by all means
> better than the grey, the average grey'. Hundertwasser
> challenged convention by using clashing colours, crooked
> windows, reflective mosaics and irregular lines in his work
> – putting his controversial stamp on everything from
> tower blocks and churches to schools and museums.

Prater

Whiffs of candy floss and the sound of merry-go-rounds fill
the air at the Prater, one of the world's oldest amusement parks.
Emperor Joseph II opened the park to the public in 1766 and kids
(not to mention big kids) still flock to the rides in droves today.
🛈 01 728 0516 🌐 www.prater.at 📧 info@wiener-prater.at
🕐 Amusement park 10.00–01.00 Mon–Sun (Mar–Oct), closed
Nov–Feb Ⓜ U-Bahn: U1 Praterstern

Riesenrad (Ferris wheel)

Vienna shrinks to the size of a postage stamp, as you climb high
in the Prater's iconic Ferris wheel. Constructed in 1897, the 65-m
(213-ft) high wheel rose to fame in the film *The Third Man* and
has been one of the city's best-loved landmarks ever since.
ⓐ Prater 🛈 01 729 5430 🌐 www.wienerriesenrad.com
📧 info@wienerriesenrad.com 🕐 09.00–24.00 Mon–Sun
(summer), 10.00–20.00 Mon–Sun (winter) Ⓜ U-Bahn: U1
Praterstern

University of Vienna Botanical Gardens

An oasis of calm, these botanical gardens nurture a variety of alpine species, plus tropical ferns, swamp plants and orchids. Unusual species to look out for include Russian olives, date plums, tubular Red buckeye flowers and Antarctic beech trees.

ⓐ Rennweg 14 ⓣ 01 427 7541 00 ⓦ www.botanik.univie.ac.at
ⓔ botanik@univie.ac.at ⓛ 09.00–dusk ⓝ S-Bahn: Rennweg

🔻 *Atelier Augarten's sculpture garden (see overleaf)*

CULTURE

Atelier Augarten (Augarten Studio)

Contemporary art enthusiasts are in their element at this light-flooded gallery, once the studio of the Austrian sculptor Gustinus Ambrosi (1893–1975), and now the home of the Österreichische Galerie Belvedere Centre for Contemporary Art. Over 2,000 stone and bronze sculptures by Ambrosi are joined by works from all over the world. Wander through the gardens to spot other abstract Austrian creations. ⓐ Scherzergasse 1a ⓣ 01 795 570 ⓦ www.atelier-augarten.at ⓛ 10.00–18.00 Tues–Sun, closed Mon (Sept–Feb); closed Mar–Aug ⓝ Tram N: Am Tabor. Admission charge

Donauwalzerhaus (Johann Strauss House)

Take a look inside the house where Strauss composed the world's most famous waltz in 1867 – *The Blue Danube*. A well-presented collection of instruments, paintings and documents traces his life.

ⓐ Praterstrasse 54 ⓣ 01 214 0121 ⓦ www.wienmuseum.at ⓛ 14.00–18.00 Tues–Thur, 10.00–13.00 Fri–Sun, closed Mon ⓝ U-Bahn: U1 Nestroyplatz. Admission charge

KunstHaus Wien

Weird, wacky and wonderful, Hundertwasser's art gallery boggles the mind. Patterned with black-and-white tiles, the façade is like a giant chessboard. Inside things get curiouser and curiouser, with uneven floors and irregular lines.

ⓐ Untere Weissgerberstrasse 13 ⓣ 01 712 0495

Ⓦ www.kunsthauswien.at Ⓛ 10.00–19.00 Mon–Sun
Ⓝ Tram N: Radetzkyplatz. Admission charge

MUK (Museum for the Art of Entertainment)

If you're strolling through the Prater, nip into this tiny museum
with its collection of circus costumes, posters and props.
Ⓐ Karmelitergasse 9 Ⓣ 01 369 1111 Ⓦ www.bezirksmuseum.at
Ⓛ 17.30–19.00 Wed, 14.30–17.00 Sat, 10.00–12.00 Sun, closed
Mon, Tue, Thur & Fri Ⓝ Tram 21: Karmeliterplatz

Österreichische Galerie Belvedere (Belvedere Gallery)

Formal gardens lead up to the rococo edifice, which houses an
amazing art collection. The palace is split into two parts: the
Upper Belvedere and the Lower Belvedere. The former
showcases 19th- and 20th-century works, including Monet and
Van Gogh masterpieces and Klimt's *Kiss*. The Lower Belvedere is
crammed with medieval, baroque and Golden Age treasures.
Ⓐ Prinz-Eugen-Strasse 37 Ⓣ 01 795 57 134 Ⓦ www.belvedere.at
Ⓔ public@belvedere.at Ⓛ 10.00–18.00 Tues–Sun, closed Mon
Ⓝ Tram D: Schloss Belvedere. Admission charge

Planetarium

Gaze at twinkling stars and far-flung galaxies in the Prater.
Using the latest laser-beam technology, the planetarium's
shows evoke an amazingly realistic universe.
Ⓐ Oswald-Thomas-Platz 1 Ⓣ 01 729 54 940 Ⓦ www.planetarium-
wien.at Ⓔ admin@planetarium-wien.at Ⓛ Shows 19.00 Fri,
15.00, 16.30, 18.00, 19.30 Sat–Sun; closed Mon–Thur Ⓝ U-Bahn: U1
Praterstern. Admission charge

Wiener Konzerthaus

This art nouveau concert hall is one of Vienna's top addresses for classical music buffs. The venue plays host to names like the Vienna Chamber Orchestra and Vienna Mozart Orchestra.

ⓐ Lothringerstrasse 20 ⓣ 01 242 002 ⓦ http://konzerthaus.at ⓔ ticket@konzerthaus.at ⓝ U-Bahn: U4 Stadtpark

RETAIL THERAPY

Burgenland Vinothek This well-stocked vaulted wine store is lined with bottles of fine Austrian Burgenland wines and liqueurs. ⓐ Baumannstrasse 3 ⓣ 01 718 2573 ⓦ www.burgenland-vinothek.at ⓛ 13.00–19.00 Tues–Fri, 10.00–17.00 Sat ⓝ U-Bahn: U3 Landstrasse-Wien Mitte

Galleria This shopping mall houses everything from Müller, C&A, Lacoste and WMF to a bookstore, nail bar and hair salon. There are also plenty of cafés and restaurants. ⓐ Landstrasser Hauptstrasse 99 ⓣ 01 712 94 72 ⓦ www.galleria-landstrasse.at ⓛ 09.00–18.30 Mon–Fri, 09.00–17.00 Sat, closed Sun ⓝ U-Bahn: U3 Station Rochusgasse

Markets

Karmelitermarkt Bustling market where the stalls are piled high with fresh fruit, vegetables and Asian specialities. ⓐ Krummbaumgasse/Leopoldsgasse ⓛ 06.00–18.30 Mon–Fri, 06.00–14.00 Sat, closed Sun ⓝ Tram 21: Karmeliterplatz

Rochusmarkt Fill your bags with fresh fruit, flowers and cheese.
ⓐ Landstrasser Hauptstrasse ● 06.00–18.30 Mon–Fri,
06.00–14.00 Sat, closed Sun ⓜ U-Bahn: U3 Rochusgasse

TAKING A BREAK

Café Meierei £ ❶ Enjoy breakfast or a light lunch on the leafy
terrace of this Prater café. Snacks include Thai stir fries and
smoked salmon with Dijon mustard. ⓐ Hauptallee 3 ⓣ 01 728
0266 ⓦ www.meierei.at ● 10.00–23.00 Mon–Sat, 09.00–22.00
Sun (summer); 11.00–19.00 Mon–Sat, 09.00–19.00 Sun (winter)
ⓜ U-Bahn: U1 Praterstern

● *Stop for lunch in a mini-jungle: KunstHaus café restaurant (overleaf)*

KunstHaus café restaurant £ Relax with a drink or snack in the KunstHaus café's lush gardens, a pocket-sized jungle complete with hanging vines, palms and flowers.
ⓐ Weissgerberlände 14 ① 01 712 0497
ⓦ www.kunsthauswien.com ① 10.00–21.00 Mon–Sun
Ⓝ U-Bahn: U1 Schwedenplatz

Tauber Café £ ❸ This café in the Galleria mall whips up great open sandwiches, from egg mayonnaise and smoked salmon to caviar and herring. ⓐ Landstrasser Hauptstrasse 99 ① 01 712 04485 ⓦ www.tauber.at ① 08.00–19.00 Mon–Fri, 08.00–18.00 Sat; closed Sun Ⓝ U-Bahn: U3 Station Rochusgasse

Lusthaus Wien ££ ❹ Surrounded by chestnut trees, this elegant baroque pavilion is the place to try lemon-and-mint Arabian iced tea with poppy cake or truffle gnocchi with parmesan. ⓐ Freudenau 254 ① 01 728 9565 ⓦ www.lusthaus-wien.at ① 12.00–23.00 Mon–Fri, 12.00–18.00 Sat–Sun (May–Sept); 12.00–18.00 Thur–Tues, closed Wed (Oct–Apr) Ⓝ U-Bahn: U3 Schlachthausgasse

AFTER DARK

Restaurants
Amon £ ❺ Set around a leafy inner courtyard, this restaurant serves dishes like monkfish on basmati and spinach-and-ricotta *knödel* (dumplings). ⓐ Schlachthausgasse 13 ① 01 798 8166 ⓦ www.amon.at ⓔ office@amon.at ① 10.00–24.00 Mon–Sat, 10.00–16.00 Sun Ⓝ U-Bahn: U3 Schlachthausgasse

Dubrovnik £ ❻ With its wood floors, stone arches and authentic Dalmatian cuisine, this restaurant is a real find. Favourites include tasty *shopska* salad and *cevapcici* (minced sausages). ⓐ Am Heumarkt 5 ❶ 01 713 7102 13 ⓦ www.dubrovnik.at ⓔ info@dubrovnik.at ❶ 11.00–15.00, 18.00–24.00 Mon–Sun ⓝ U-Bahn: U4 Stadtpark

Kolariks Himmelreich £ ❼ In the heart of the Prater, this relaxed restaurant with an attractive beer garden offers good value, no-nonsense fare. ⓐ Waldsteingartenstrasse 128 ❶ 01 729 49 9974 ⓦ www.kolarik.at ⓔ office@kolarik.at ❶ 11.00–24.00 Mon–Sat, 11.00–23.00 Sun ⓝ U-Bahn: U1 Praterstern

Salm Bräu £ ❽ Sample homebrews and Viennese fare at this brewery restaurant. The meaty menu features Bohemian beer soup, pork shank and smoked venison ham. Take a pew in the 17th-century Georgsaal or red-brick cellar vault. ⓐ Rennweg 8 ❶ 01 799 5992 ⓦ www.salmbraeu.com ❶ 11.00–24.00 Mon–Sun ⓝ Tram 71: Unteres Belverdere

Taverna Lefteris £ ❾ Greek restaurant with a rustic feel. Savour Cretan cuisine including mezze, moussaka or marinated octopus salad with a glass of Retsina. ⓐ Hörnesgasse 17 ❶ 01 7137 451 ⓦ www.taverna-lefteris.at ⓔ taverna-lefteris@chello.at ❶ 18.00–24.00 Mon–Sat, closed Sun ⓝ U-Bahn: U3 Rochusgasse

Wieselburger Bierinsel £ ❿ This cheery Prater restaurant has free-flowing beer and a shady terrace where you can tuck into huge steaks barbecued over lava stone or spicy Viennese

goulash. ⓐ Prater 11 ⓣ 01 729 4785 ⓦ www.bierinsel.at
ⓛ 08.30–23.00 Mon–Sun ⓝ U-Bahn: U1 Praterstern

Restaurant Vincent ££ ⑪ Foodies go gaga over Gerold Kulterer's
award-winning cuisine. Decked out in blacks and creams, the
décor is minimalist chic and the service snappy. The scallops, trout
with almonds and Bresse chicken come recommended.
ⓐ Grosse Pfarrgasse 7 ⓣ 01 214 1516 ⓦ www.restaurant-vincent.at
ⓔ office@restaurant-vincent.at ⓛ 18.00–24.00 Mon–Sat, closed
Sun ⓝ U-Bahn: U3 Landstrasse-Wien Mitte

Bars & clubs

Arena Ear-splitting music rocks the crowd at this popular club
which stages rock, metal and punk concerts. There's an open-air
cinema in summer. ⓐ Baumgasse 80 ⓣ 01 798 8595
ⓦ www.arena.co.at ⓝ U-Bahn: U3 Erdberg

Birdland Sounds of the saxophone fill this smooth jazz club in
the Hilton hotel's basement. ⓐ Am Stadtpark 1 ⓣ 01 588 85
ⓦ www.birdland.at ⓛ 18.00–02.00 Tues–Sun, closed Mon
ⓝ U-Bahn: U3 Landstrasse-Wien Mitte

Club Massiv DJs from the far corners of the globe spin techno and
house grooves at this offbeat cellar in the 3rd district. Serious
clubbers can dance here till dawn. ⓐ Untere Weissgerberstrasse
37 ⓣ 01 714 51 45 ⓦ www.massiv.at ⓛ 18.00–open end Mon–Sun
ⓔ office@massiv.at ⓝ Tram N: Hetzgasse

ⓞ *Terraced vineyards are a feature of the Danube Valley*

OUT OF TOWN
trips

Wienerwald

Visualise vine-clad hills riddled with caves and limestone cliffs sprinkled with Benedictine abbeys. This UNESCO Biosphere Reserve is a gorgeous pocket of greenery ranging from shady oak forests to Roman spas, vaulted wineries to rare wildlife. Although just a stone's throw from the capital, Vienna's wild and wonderful backyard feels a million miles from the centre's buzz.

If you're looking to add a natural twist and a touch of escapism to your short break to Vienna, the picturesque Wienerwald hits the spot, from scaling gorges to climbing centuries-old fortresses. Hire bikes to cycle through tree-fringed nature reserves or hike the Via Sacra for a cultural overdose.

◆ *Burg Wildegg*

Whether you want all-out action or plenty of pampering, if you go down to Vienna's woods today, you're sure of a big surprise.

GETTING THERE

Bordering west Vienna, the Wienerwald is easy to access. The A1 motorway runs to Pressbaum in 30 minutes, while the A21 connects towns like Hinterbrühl, Heiligenkreuz and Alland. Frequent ÖBB train and bus connections link Westbahnhof station to most towns and villages. The regional public transport network provides timetable details. Ⓦ www.vor.at

SIGHTS AND ATTRACTIONS

Allander Tropfsteinhöhle

Tucked into Buchenberg mountain, these 70-m (230-ft) long dripstone caves are a paleontological site. Don sturdy footwear to look at stalactites, stalagmites and the 10,000-year-old remains of a brown bear.

ⓐ Buchberg/Alland Ⓣ 02258 6666 Ⓦ www.alland.at Ⓛ 10.00–17.00 Sat–Sun (Apr–Oct); 13.00–17.00 Mon–Fri (July–Aug); closed Nov–Mar Ⓝ Bus: 365. Admission charge

Burg Wildegg

Hike up to this medieval castle surrounded by thick woodlands. The castle's lofty turrets and fortified walls loom large over the valley.

ⓐ Sittendorf Ⓣ 01 51552 3395 (Vienna info) ⓔ wildegg@jungschar.at Ⓝ Bus: 364

Vienna region

0 — 2 km
0 — 2 miles

Vienna region

Austria

Zwettl

Rastenfeld

Gföhl

Ottenschlag

Dürnstein

Krems

Weißenkirchen

Mautern
an der Donau

Spitz

Stift Göttweig

Pöggstall

Aggsbach
Markt

B3

Artstetten

Grein

B3

Maria Taferl

Donau
(Danube)

Melk

St Pölten

Ybbs
an der Donau

A1

B1

Linz
Airport

Amstetten

Mank

Kirchberg
an der Pielach

Waidhofen
an der Ybbs

Scheibbs

Lilienfeld

B20

Annaberg

N

Göstling
an der Ybbs

Mariazell

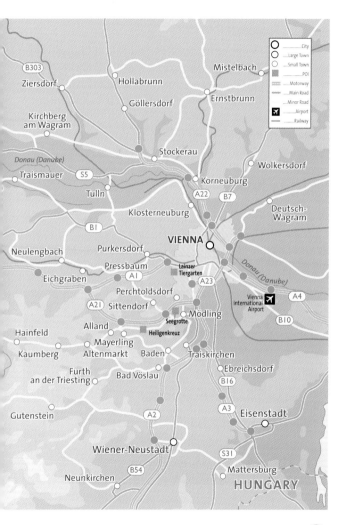

Dreidärrischenhöhle

Tread carefully in the eerie *Dreidärrischenhöhle*, or 'cave of the three madmen'. Keep quiet to spot the four species of endangered bats living here. The cave was unearthed in the 19th century, but closed when World War II broke out. It's now free to visit.

ⓐ Gaaden ⓦ www.showcaves.com ⓛ Apr–Oct, closed Nov–Mar
ⓝ Bus: 365

Föhrenberge Nature Reserve

Marked trails attract walkers and cyclists to this park's limestone crags, open moors and heathland. Look out for umbrella trees, black pines and red squirrels.

ⓐ Perchtoldsdorf ⓣ 02236 28796 ⓦ www.naturparke.at
ⓝ S-Bahn: S9; Bus: 260

🔺 *The church and hunting lodge at Mayerling*

Heiligenkreuz

Think *The Sound of Music* and this picture-perfect Cistercian abbey won't disappoint. Elegant spires rise above the red-roofed structure, sitting on 900 years of history. Seek out the church's Romanesque cloister, cross-ribbed vaulting and the Fountain House's Babenberg family portraits.

ⓐ Heiligenkreuz ⓣ 02258 8703 ⓦ www.stift-heiligenkreuz.org
ⓛ 10.00–16.00 Mon–Sat, closed Sun ⓝ Bus: 365.
Admission charge

Jagdschloss Mayerling (Mayerling Lodge)

This former royal hunting lodge is where Crown Prince Rudolf and his 17-year-old mistress Baroness Marie Vetsera were found dead in 1889. The exhibition reveals more about the famous murder mystery.

ⓐ Mayerling, Alland ⓣ 02258 2275 ⓛ 09.00–12.30, 13.30–17.00 Mon–Sun ⓝ Bus: 365/458

Klosterneuburg

Perched high above the Danube, the mighty spires and domes of this Benedictine abbey are a sight to behold. Step inside to uncover the giant baroque organ, centuries-old wine cellars and the astonishing 12th-century altarpiece, painted in 51 panels over a period of 10 years by Nicholas of Verdun – it's one of the world's finest medieval artworks.

ⓐ Stiftsplatz 1, Klosterneuburg ⓣ 02243 4110
ⓦ www.stift-klosterneuburg.at ⓝ Bus: 202.
Admission charge

Leopold-Figl-Warte

This bizarre-looking corkscrew tower set on the top of the 494-m (1,621-ft) high Tulbinger Kogel mountain twists to a viewing platform that peers above the treetops. On a clear day you'll get fine views of the Danube, Krems and the alpine peaks of Ötscher, Rax and Schneeberg.

ⓐ Tulbinger Kogel Ⓝ Bus: 449

Sandstein Nature Reserve

A shady beech forest with a game reserve and nature trails, this expanse of greenery is the place to come eye-to-eye with free-roaming deer and wild boar. Follow the path to the highest point, 475-m (1,560-ft) Rudolfshöhe, for far-reaching views over the Wienerwald and Vienna. Children love the animal petting area.

ⓐ Purkersdorf ⓣ 02231 627 46 Ⓦ www.purkersdorf.at
Ⓝ S-Bahn: S50

> ### HOLY HILLS
> A magnet for hikers and bikers, the Via Sacra trail weaves from Vienna to Mariazell along a path used by pilgrims over centuries. Crossing meadows, forest and low mountains, and featuring many shrines along the way, the Wienerwald's 29-km (18-mile) stretch passes through Gaaden, Heiligenkreuz, Alland and Kaumberg. The trek is a great way to slip under the region's skin and discover highlights like Gaaden's twin-domed church, the Cistercian abbey of Heiligenkreuz and Alland's dripstone caves. ⓣ 02237 7203 Ⓦ www.via-sacra.at

Seegrotte Hinterbrühl

This former mine became Europe's largest subterranean lake in 1912 when it was accidentally flooded with 20 m litres (4.4 m gallons) of water. Weave through narrow mining tunnels and see the cobalt blue lake shimmer far below ground.

ⓐ Grutschgasse 2a, Hinterbrühl ⓣ 02236 26 364
ⓦ www.seegrotte.at ⓛ 09.00–17.00 Mon–Sun (Apr–Oct); 09.00–12.00, 13.00–15.00 Mon–Fri, 09.00–15.30 Sat–Sun (Nov–Mar) ⓝ Bus: 364/365. Admission charge

Steinwandklamm

Steep steps climb this precipitous gorge, with its silvery waterfalls and moss-covered boulders. The 45-minute trek is

⬥ Heiligenkreuz (see page 109)

pleasant even in the summer, as temperatures hover around
10°C (50°F). Don't attempt it with a pushchair!

ⓐ Furth an der Triesting ⓣ 02674 88219 ⓦ www.
furth-triesting.at ⓛ Apr–Oct, closed Nov–Mar ⓝ Bus: 556

CULTURE

Stadttheater Baden

This 18th-century theatre stages quality ballet, opera, theatre
and musicals. The Sommerarena takes over during the summer.

ⓐ Theaterplatz 7, Baden ⓣ 02252 48 547
ⓦ www.stadttheater-baden.at ⓔ ticket@stadttheater-baden.at
ⓛ Sept–Apr, closed May–Aug ⓝ Bus: 360

Wienerwaldmuseum

Culture vultures trace the Wienerwald back to Neolithic times
at this intriguing museum housed in a former farm, which
contains everything from Iron Age coins to Roman jewellery.
A highlight is the convincing cave reproduction.

ⓐ Hauptstrasse 17, Eichgraben ⓣ 02773 46904
ⓦ www.wienerwaldmuseum.at ⓛ 08.00–11.00 Wed–Thur,
14.00–17.00 Sat, 10.00–12.00, 14.00–17.00 Sun, closed Mon &
Tues, Fri ⓝ Train: Eichgraben-Altlengbach. Admission charge

RECREATION

Lainzer Tiergarten

This expansive conservation area on the edge of Vienna is
perfect for a picnic amidst undisturbed nature. Stroll past beech

and oak trees to spot wild boar, moufflon and deer. Look out for endangered species including the white-backed woodpecker and fire salamander.

ⓐ Lainzer Tor, 13 Hermesstrasse ❶ 01 804 3169
Ⓦ www.wien.gv.at 🕓 09.00–17.00 (winter); 08.00–20.00 (summer) Ⓝ Tram: 60

Römertherme Baden

Take the therapeutic waters at Baden's thermal spa and sauna complex. The glass-roofed pool features bubbly whirlpools, massage jets and underwater music to help you drift away. Steam in 95°C (203°F) Finnish saunas and herbal baths, or unwind with a massage in the beauty centre. ⓐ Brusattiplatz 4, Baden ❶ 02252 45030 Ⓦ www.roemertherme.at 🕓 10.00–22.00 Mon–Sun Ⓝ Bus: 360. Admission charge

Thermalbad Bad Vöslau

Even the beauty-conscious Romans knew the benefits of Bad Vöslau's thermal springs. Nowadays you can take a dip in 26°C (46°F) waters, test out red-hot Nordic saunas, or get active with volleyball and tennis. ⓐ Badenerstrasse, Bad Vöslau ❶ 02252 762660 Ⓦ www.thermalbad-voeslau.at 🕓 08.00–19.00 Mon–Sun (Apr–Oct); 08.00–20.00 Mon–Sun (June–Aug); closed Nov–Mar Ⓝ Train: Bad Vöslau. Admission charge

Weinstrasse Thermenregion

Hear corks pop on the Wienerwald's wine route. The loop takes in 22 wine-growing villages and spa towns like Perchtoldsdorf, Baden, Sollenau and Tattendorf. Sniff out spicy Zierfandler and

zesty Rotgipfler whites in wineries peppering the gently sloping vineyards. ❶ 02252 70743 Ⓦ www.weinstrassen.at

RETAIL THERAPY

Badener Hauervinothek The shelves are lined with 100 local wines at this medieval-style store with vaulted ceilings and tasting tables where you can try before you buy. Pick up a bottle of the burning homemade schnapps. ⓐ Brusattiplatz 2, Baden ❶ 02252 456 40 Ⓦ www.hauervinothek.at Ⓛ 10.00–12.30, 15.00–18.30 Mon–Sun Ⓝ Bus: 360

Made by You Choose a handthrown pot, plate or vase at this quirky ceramics workshop, then get painting. There's everything here to create your own mini-masterpiece. ⓐ Antonsgasse 14, Baden ❶ 02252 252 186 Ⓦ www.madebyyou.at ⓔ malen@madebyyou.at Ⓛ 10.00–12.30, 15.00–18.00 Mon–Thur, 10.00–12.30, 15.00–19.00 Fri, 10.00–17.00 Sat, closed Sun Ⓝ Bus: 360

TAKING A BREAK

Backhaus Annamühle £ Cosy café with pastries, coffee and light lunches in the courtyard. ⓐ Heiligenkreuzergasse 3–5, Baden ❶ 02252 123 456 Ⓦ www.backhaus-annamuehle.at Ⓛ 05.30–18.00 Mon–Fri, 05.30–12.00 Sat, closed Sun Ⓝ Bus: 360

Café Central £ This relaxed, wood-panelled Viennese café has served the residents of central Baden for 200 years. Warm up

with creamy pumpkin soup or a rum-laced mocha with apple strudel. ❷ Hauptplatz 19, Baden ❶ 02252 484 54 ❼ www.café-central.at ❿ 07.00–21.00 Tues–Sat, 08.00–21.00 Sun, closed Mon ❻ Bus: 360

Elf'is Radlertreff £ A beloved pit-stop of cyclists, this snack bar is the place to refresh with a draught Fohrenburger beer, slurp homemade goulash soup and surf the web. ❷ Flugfeldstrasse 40, Bad Vöslau ❶ 02252 78858 ❼ www.radlertreff.at ❿ 11.30–20.00 Tues–Sun, closed Mon ❻ Train: Bad Vöslau

Klostergasthof Heiligenkreuz £ After visiting the abbey, rest beside fountains in the courtyard or take a pew in the beamed restaurant for fresh salads and game specialities with a glass of Grauer Mönch wine. Children's menus are available. ❷ Heiligenkreuz ❶ 02258 8703 138 ❼ www.klostergasthof-heiligenkreuz.at ❿ 09.00–22.00 Mon–Sun ❻ Bus: 365

AFTER DARK

Restaurants

Gasthaus Mirli £ Worth a detour, this farmhouse set in orchards tempts with creative cuisine using fresh local fare. Savour saffron-coconut shrimps on black spaghetti or pheasant in pepper sauce. ❷ Heinratsberg 69, Irenental ❶ 0664 222 3131 ❼ www.mirli.at ❺ info@mirli.at ❿ 11.30–22.00 Wed–Sun, closed Mon–Tues ❻ Bus: 351/408

Panorama Restaurant £ Laid-back restaurant with a lantern-lit terrace, views of the Wienerwald and hearty Austrian fare like beef soup with profiteroles. ⓐ Gumpoldskirchnerstrasse 50, Mödling ⓣ 02236 24541 ⓦ www.panoramarestaurant.at ⓔ office@panoramarestaurant.at ⓛ 11.00–23.00 Mon–Sun ⓝ U-Bahn: U6; S-Bahn: S9 Mödling

Florians ££ Terracotta hues, wood floors and modern art set the scene for fusion flavours like pumpkin risotto and roast pork in chorizo sauce in this smart restaurant. ⓐ Neudorferstrasse 68, Mödling ⓣ 02236 892 454 ⓦ www.florians.at ⓔ essen@florians.at ⓛ 11.30–14.00, 18.00–22.00 Tue–Sat, closed Sun & Mon ⓝ U-Bahn: U6; S-Bahn: S9 Mödling

Höldrichsmühle ££ Dine in the historic vaults of this 18th-century corn mill. Pull up a chair on the terrace beside the stream to enjoy fresh trout or game ragout with Austrian wines. ⓐ Gaadnerstrasse 34, Hinterbrühl ⓣ 02236 26 2740 ⓦ www.hoeldrichsmuehle.at ⓔ hoeld@eunet.at ⓛ 07.00–23.00 Mon–Sun ⓝ Bus: 364/365

Trattoria Dazanini ££ A gem of an Italian restaurant where the menu is small but everything is cooked to perfection. Tuck into antipasti, red snapper and raspberry pannacotta. ⓐ Hauptstrasse 65, Mödling ⓣ 0664 545 1046 ⓦ www.dazanini.com ⓔ trattoria@dazanini.com ⓛ 12.00–15.00, 18.00–23.00 Tue–Fri, 11.00–15.00 Sat, closed Sun–Mon ⓝ U-bahn: U6; S-Bahn: S9 Mödling

The Wachau Valley

Whether you fancy sipping fruity Rieslings on a gently sloping vine-clad hillside or cruising the snaking River Danube, getting giddy on the top of a medieval fortress or gawping at Benedictine abbeys, the Wachau Valley offers rich pickings. A heady mix of world-class culture and natural highs, this UNESCO World Heritage Site beckons – explore it on foot, by bike, or accompanied by a llama...

While many people flit past en route to Vienna, it's worth lingering to explore the hidden nooks of this Eden-like valley that wears every season well. In summer, boats chugging along the river reveal snapshot views of gravity-defying castles, in autumn vines kindle into colour and apple orchards hang heavy, while winter is time to retreat to a cosy *Heurige* (wine cellar) to relax with a glass of Grüner Veltliner by an open fire. Sounds tempting? It is.

⬤ *Aggstein, perched on cliffs overlooking the Danube Valley*

GETTING THERE

The A22 and S5 motorways link Vienna to the Wachau Valley, an hour's drive away. There are frequent train connections between the Wesbahnhof and towns like Krems (1 hr 10 mins), Melk (1 hr 20 mins) and Ybbs (1 hr 30 mins). ÖBB buses operate an efficient regional service.

SIGHTS & ATTRACTIONS

Aggstein

Clinging to wooded cliffs, this gravity-defying 12th-century fortress affords precipitous views over the Danube Valley. Steep wooden steps lead up to the silver-turreted castle, which was destroyed in 1296 and rebuilt during Renaissance times.
ⓐ Aggsbach ⓣ 02753 82 281 ⓦ www.ruineaggstein.at
ⓔ info@ruineaggstein.at ⓛ 09.00–18.00 (Apr–Oct), closed Nov–Mar ⓝ Bus: 1451. Admission charge

Burg Dürnstein

A rocky path twists up to these medieval ruins, where Richard the Lionheart was held prisoner until he was freed by his minstrel Blondel. Towering over the pastel-washed town of Dürnstein, the castle has fairytale appeal and sweeping river views.
ⓐ Dürnstein ⓣ 0340 646 150 ⓦ www.duernstein.at ⓣ 02711 200
ⓝ Train: Dürnstein-Oberloiben

Maria Taferl Basilica

The domed towers of this baroque basilica, illuminated by

night, are a shrine to pilgrims. The church is still being renovated, but inside you can admire Antonio Beduzzi's ceiling frescoes and the gilded treasure chamber. The Celtic *opferstein* (sacrifice rock) sits in the square.

ⓐ Maria Taferl 1 ☏ 07413 278 0 ⓦ www.basilika.at
ⓔ info@basilika.at Ⓝ Bus: 7721

Schloss Artstetten

This onion-domed palace towers high above parkland. Once the Habsburgs' summer residence, it is the final resting place of Crown Prince Franz Ferdinand and Sophie, Duchess of Hohenberg. The museum's exhibition traces Franz Ferdinand's life.

ⓐ Artstetten ☏ 07413 80 060 ⓦ www.schloss-artstetten.at
ⓔ museum@schloss-artstetten.at ⏲ 09.00–17.30 (Apr–Oct), closed Nov–Mar Ⓝ Bus: 1462. Admission charge

Stift Göttweig

Founded by St Altmann, Bishop of Passau, in 1083, this Benedictine monastery perching high on a hill above the Danube Valley has been dubbed the Austrian Monte Cassino.

ⓐ Furth ☏ 02732 855 81 231 ⓦ www.stiftgoettweig.or.at
ⓔ tourismus@stiftgoettweig.at ⏲ 10.00–18.00 (Mar–Nov), closed Dec–Feb Ⓝ Bus: 112. Admission charge

Stift Melk

This breathtaking yellow-and-white Benedictine abbey rises like a vision above the Danube. Be inspired by the gold-hued library and Paul Trogers' frescoes in the Marble Hall. In summer, wander past fountains and linden trees in the landscape garden.

Abt Berthold Dietmayrstrasse 1, Melk 02752 555 225
www.stiftmelk.at 09.00–18.00 (summer); 09.00–17.00
(winter) Train: Melk. Admission charge

Tausend-Eimer Berg

Dominating Spitz, this vine-clad hill is nicknamed 1,000-Bucket
Mountain because of the amount of wine it can supposedly
yield. Tumbling down to the banks of the Danube, the steep
terraces produce some of the region's finest Rieslings. Views
from here are pretty intoxicating too.

Spitz www.spitz-wachau.at Train: Spitz

CULTURE

Krems Kunstmeile

Art buffs make a beeline for Krems' cultural mile, taking in
highlights such as the glass-roofed Kunsthalle, which displays
contemporary works alongside Biedermeier masterpieces, the
Caricature Museum and a string of other workshops and galleries.

Krems 02732 90 8000 www.kunstmeile.cc
info@kunstmeile.cc Train: Krems. Admission charge

Römermuseum

The town of Mautern goes back to its Roman roots at this
intriguing museum with a collection of artefacts unearthed
in the 1930s. Look out for the reconstructed kitchen.

Schlossgasse 12, Mautern 02732 81155 www.mautern.at
10.00–12.00 Wed–Sun, 16.00–18.00 Fri–Sat, closed Mon–Tues
Train: Stein-Mautern. Admission charge

Weinstadtmuseum Krems

Housed in a 13th-century Dominican monastery, this heritage museum houses viticulture-related artefacts, Gothic sculptures and the tiny 32,000-year-old Fanny vom Galgenberg statuette, Austria's oldest artwork.

🅐 Körnermarkt 14, Krems 🅣 02732 801567
🅦 www.weinstadtmuseum.at 🅛 10.00–18.00 Tues–Sun, closed Mon (Mar–Nov); closed Dec–Feb 🅝 Train: Krems. Admission charge

🔺 *Burg Dürnstein clings to the rocky hillside above Dürnstein*

RECREATION

Blue Danube Cruise

Cruise the Danube to soak up the Wachau Valley's sights from the water. You can buy tickets for the two-hour, 36-km (22-mile) tour from Krems to Melk onboard. Shorter trips are also available. ⓐ Friedrichstrasse 7, Vienna (info centre) ⓣ 01 588 80 ⓦ www.ddsg-blue-danube.at ⓔ info@ddsg-blue-danube.at

Kellerschlössel der Freien Weingärtner

Savour home-grown wines like Grüner Veltliner and Zweigelt at Dürnstein's age-old cellars. ⓐ Dürnstein ⓣ 02711 371 ⓦ www.fww.at ⓛ 09.00–18.00 Mon–Sat, 10.00–16.00 Sun (Apr–Oct) ⓝ Train: Dürnstein-Oberloiben. Admission charge

Llama Trekking

A trekking tour with a South American twist, this two-day llama trek from Göttweig to Melk passes through the Dunkelsteinerwald forest and pauses at Maria Langegg monastery, where you spend the night. The Donau Tourist Office provides details. ⓐ Schlossgasse 3, Spitz (info centre) ⓣ 02713 300 6060 ⓦ www.donau.com ⓔ urlaub@donau.com

Rent a Wachau Bike

A well-marked cycling path follows the River Danube through the Wachau Valley. This store rents mountain, city and children's bikes at fair rates, and can deliver them to your hotel. ⓐ Austrasse 50, Mautern ⓣ 0664 214 3512 ⓕ 02732 78617 ⓦ www.rentawachaubike.at

RETAIL THERAPY

Kalt Eis 21 Splurge on designer jewellery from strings of pearls to Armani watches. ⓐ Obere Landstrasse 21, Krems ⓣ 02732 70647 ⓦ www.kalteis-21.at ⓔ info@kalteis-21.at ⓛ 10.00–13.00 Mon, 10.00–13.00, 15.00–18.00 Tues–Fri, 09.00–13.00 Sat, closed Sun ⓝ Train: Krems

Wein Handlung Noitz im Kloster Follow your nose to find (and taste) Austria's biggest selection of wines. ⓐ Undstrasse 6, Krems-Stein ⓣ 02732 856 564 ⓦ www.wein-handlung.at ⓛ 11.00–19.00 Wed–Sun, closed Mon–Tues (May–Oct); 11.00–19.00 Tues–Sat, closed Sun–Mon (Nov–Apr) ⓝ Train: Krems

Wieser Shiny bottles and jars line shelves at this foodie enclave, selling specialities like plum schnapps, pumpkin and ginger marmalades, chutneys, oils, chocolate, coffee, wine and natural cosmetics. ⓐ Altstadt 39, Dürnstein ⓣ 02711 80544 ⓦ www.wieser-online.at ⓔ duernstein@wieser-online.at ⓛ 08.30–18.00 Mon–Sun ⓝ Train: Dürnstein-Oberloiben

TAKING A BREAK

Babenbergerhof £ Relax with a light lunch and glass of wine on this manor's cobbled courtyard. The daily menu offers excellent value. ⓐ Wienerstrasse 10, Ybbs ⓣ 0741 254 334 ⓦ www.babenbergerhof.at ⓔ office@babenbergerhof.at ⓝ Train: Ybbs

Café Hagmann Krems £ A snug café with delicious handmade pralines and pastries. ⓐ Untere Landstrasse 8, Krems ❶ 02732 83167 ⓦ www.hagmann.co.at ⓛ 07.00–18.30 Mon–Fri, 07.00–17.00 Sat, 13.30–18.00 Sun ⓝ Train: Krems

Café Restaurant zum Fürsten £ Dark-wood panelling and low lighting create an old-world feel in this café on the square. Browse newspapers as you munch snacks with gallons of strong coffee. ⓐ Rathausplatz 3, Melk ❶ 02752 52343 ⓔ café.madar@netway.at ⓝ Train: Melk

AFTER DARK

Restaurants
Florianihof £ Draped in vines, this 14th-century manor serves creative flavours in the vaulted cellar and on the terrace. ⓐ Wösendorf 74, Weissenkirchen ❶ 02715 2212 ⓦ www.florianihof-wachau.at ⓛ 12.00–14.30, 18.00–21.30 Mon, Tues & Fri, 12.00–21.30 Sat & Sun, closed Wed & Thur ⓝ Train: Weissenkirchen

Gozzoburg £ Peering over red rooftops, this restaurant dates back to medieval times. The décor is rustic, the vibe relaxed and the food good value – try the flavoursome herring salad. ⓐ Margaretenstrasse 14, Krems ❶ 02732 85247 ⓦ www.gozzoburg-krems.at ⓛ 11.00–24.00 Wed–Mon, closed Tues ⓝ Train: Krems

Loibnerhof £ Four hundred-year-old restaurant with lanterns to illuminate the huge tree-fringed terrace. Savour specialities like Wachau fish soup, homemade goose liver pâté and nut schnapps. ⓐ Unterloiben 7, Dürnstein ☏ 02732 828 900 ⓦ www.loibnerhof.at ⓔ office@loibnerhof.at ⏰ 11.30–24.00 Wed–Sun, closed Mon–Tues Ⓝ Train: Dürnstein-Oberloiben

Bacher ££ Michelin flavours leave you starry eyed at this gourmet haunt. Book a table in advance to feast on beautifully presented dishes in the garden or beside the Kaminstüberl's open fire. There are ten comfortable bedrooms if you decide to make a night of it. ⓐ Südtirolerplatz 2, Mautern ☏ 02732 82 937 ⓦ www.landhaus-bacher.at ⓔ info@landhaus-bacher.at ⏰ 11.30–14.00, 18.30–21.30 Wed–Sun, closed Mon & Tues Ⓝ Bus: Mautern

Weingut Holzapfel ££ Dine alfresco on the inner courtyard framed by palms and oleander bushes at this award-winning winery. The home-smoked ham and brook trout in Riesling sauce come recommended. ⓐ Joching 36, Weissenkirchen ☏ 02715 2310 ⓦ www.holzapfel.at ⓔ weingut@holzapfel.at ⏰ 11.30–22.30 Wed–Sat, 11.30–15.00 Sun, closed Mon & Tues Ⓝ Train: Weissenkirchen

ACCOMMODATION

Gästehaus Heller £ Well located for long hikes through the vines, this cheery hotel offers spotless, light-flooded rooms with satellite TV. Chill out in the peaceful garden and enjoy views over Dürnstein. ⓐ Kremser Strasse 14, Weissenkirchen ☏ 0271 52221 Ⓝ Train: Weissenkirchen

Junges Hotel Dolce Vita £ The best budget deal in town, this youth hostel with dorms and private rooms is 5-star roughing it. There's handy stuff like internet access, a bike garage, barbecue area, cafeteria and lounge. ⓐ Abt Karl Strasse 42, Melk ⓣ 02752 526 81 ⓦ www.noejhw.at ⓔ melk@noejhw.at ⓝ Train: Melk

Marbacher Campingplatz £ Pitch a tent at this leafy campsite which overlooks the Danube and doubles as a watersports centre. Nearby activities include golf, tennis, cycling and waterskiing. ⓐ Marbach ⓣ 07413 207 33 ⓔ info@marbach-freizeit.at ⓛ Apr–Oct, closed Nov–Mar ⓝ Bus: 7721

Orange Wings £ This no-nonsense contemporary hotel with comfy king-size beds, 24-hour check-in and free high-speed internet access makes up for in value and convenience what it lacks in character. ⓐ Hofrat Erben Strasse 4, Krems ⓣ 02732 780 04 ⓦ www.orangewings.com ⓔ krems@orangewings.com ⓝ Train: Krems

Barock-Landhof Burkhardt ££ This 16th-century manor screams posh, but rates are surprisingly affordable. Stroll through rose gardens and orchards in the rambling grounds, or stop to admire the ivy-clad courtyard. The spacious rooms have minibar, satellite TV and mountain or river views. ⓐ Kremser Strasse 19, Spitz ⓣ 02713 2356 ⓦ www.barock-landhof.de ⓔ info@burkhardt.at ⓝ Train: Spitz

---

◗ *The central Tourist Office on the corner of Albertinaplatz and Maysedergasse*

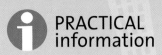

PRACTICAL
information

Directory

GETTING THERE

By air

A number of airlines operate a frequent, direct service between Vienna International Airport and European destinations like London, Paris, Cologne, Amsterdam and Berlin, including budget airlines like Germanwings and Air Berlin. A 20-minute journey from the centre, the modern airport offers a full range of services including ATMs, shops and currency exchange. Ryanair flies from London Stansted to Bratislava, 60 km (36 miles) from Vienna (transfer by bus takes around 90 minutes).

Air Berlin ⓦ www.air-berlin.com

Ryanair ⓦ www.ryanair.com

Germanwings ⓦ www13.germanwings.com

Many people are aware that air travel emits CO_2, which contributes to climate change. You may be interested in lessening the environmental impact of your flight through the charity Climate Care, which offsets your CO_2 by funding environmental projects around the world. Visit ⓦ www.climatecare.org

By car

Austria's roads and motorways are well maintained. Driving is on the right and international signs are used. If possible, it's wise to avoid rush hour (7.30am–9am and 4pm–6pm) when roads can get congested. On a clear run you can reach Bratislava in an hour, Graz in two hours and Salzburg in three hours.

By rail

If you travel by train to Vienna, you'll arrive at Südbahnhof or Westbahnhof. Austria's national rail network ÖBB runs an efficient service to major cities including Salzburg, Innsbruck and Linz, plus international destinations like Berlin, Paris, Munich, Basel and Bratislava. The ÖBB website provides details on timetables and bookings. **ÖBB** Ⓦ www.oebb.at

By bus

National Express and Eurolines operate a service between Vienna and a number of European destinations. Most international and long-distance buses pull into central bus stations like Landstrasse/Wien Mitte, Südbahnhof and Schwedenplatz. **National Express** Ⓦ www.nationalexpress.com **Eurolines** Ⓦ www.eurolines.com

ENTRY FORMALITIES
Documentation

EU, Australian, Canadian, New Zealand and United States citizens must have a valid passport to enter Austria, but do not require a visa for stays of less than 90 days. If you are arriving from another country, you may need a visa and should contact your consulate or embassy before departure. The Austrian Foreign Ministry provides more information on entry requirements. Ⓦ www.bmaa.gv.at

CUSTOMS

It is free to import goods worth up to €175 from a non-EU country, but you should check restrictions on the imports of tobacco, perfume and alcohol. EU residents can import 800 cigarettes, 1 kg of tobacco, 10 litres of spirits, 90 litres of wine and 110 litres of beer for personal use. Further information is available at Ⓦ www.bmf.gov.at

MONEY

The national currency is the euro (€), broken down into 100 cents. One euro is roughly equivalent to £0.65 or $1.25. Coins are in denominations of 1, 2, 5, 10, 20 and 50 cents, and of 1 and 2 euros. There are banknotes of 5, 10, 20, 50, 100, 200 and 500 euros.

There are plenty of ATMs in central Vienna where you can withdraw cash with a credit or debit card 24 hours a day. Banks are normally open 08.00–15.00 Mon–Wed and Fri, and 08.00–17.30 Thur. You'll find bureaux de change in banks, airports and the main station. Banks usually offer the best currency exchange rates. Most bureaux de change, travel agencies and hotels accept euro traveller's cheques for cashing.

HEALTH, SAFETY & CRIME

It is generally safe to visit Vienna and there are no particular health risks. No immunisations or health certificates are required, and the tap water is safe to drink.

Austria has a very high standard of medical care. Pharmacies (*Apotheken*) can give medical advice and treat minor ailments and are usually open 08.00–18.00 Mon–Fri and 08.00–12.00 Sat. Your hotel should be able to arrange for you to see an English-speaking doctor, if necessary.

EU citizens are entitled to free or reduced-cost emergency health care in Austria with a valid European Health Insurance Card (EHIC), which entitles you to state medical treatment but does not cover repatriation or long-term illness. There is a charge for routine medical care. All travellers should invest in a good health insurance policy before visiting.

For a city of its size, the crime rate in Vienna is low. However, it's wise to keep an eye on your belongings in crowded areas where pickpockets might lurk. If you are the victim of a crime, you should inform the police by calling 133 (see *Emergencies*, pages 138–9).

OPENING HOURS
Shops
The centre's main shops and malls generally open 09.00–18.30 Mon–Fri and 09.00–18.00 Sat. Many stay open until 21.00 on Thursday and Friday for late-night shopping. Souvenir shops, bakeries and the shopping centres at Westbahnhof and Südbahnhof stations open on Sunday.

Banks
Banks generally open 08.00–15.00 Mon–Wed and Fri, and 08.00–17.30 Thur. Most close at weekends, but many in the city centre have 24-hour ATMs. The banks at Westbahnhof station (07.00–22.00) and Vienna International Airport (08.00–23.00) open daily.

Post offices
Most post offices open 08.00–12.00 and 14.00–18.00 Mon–Fri, and some 08.00–10.00 Sat. Vienna's main post office on Fleischmarkt and those located at Westbahnhof, Südbahnhof and Franz-Josefs-Bahnhof stations stay open 24 hours.

TOILETS

Practically every station, square and street corner has a WC.
Keep some spare change handy (usually €0.40) to open
the door or tip the attendant. Most conveniences are
accessible for travellers with disabilities and have a baby-
changing area.

CHILDREN

From climbing the sky in the Prater's giant Ferris wheel to
creating their own waltz in the House of Music, this child-
friendly city is one place little ones will want to stay. Attractions
usually offer a 50 per cent reduction for children. Most
department stores and public toilets have clean baby-changing
facilities, including the public conveniences at Schwedenplatz,
Stephansplatz and Volksprater.

Naturhistorische Museum (Natural History Museum) Budding
explorers can go back to the year dot to unearth dinosaur
skeletons, fossils and minerals in this fun-fuelled museum with
an educational twist. ⓐ Burgring 7 ⓦ www.nhm-wien.ac.at
ⓔ homepage@nhm-wien.ac.at ⓛ 09.00–18.30 Wed–Mon,
closed Tues ⓝ U-Bahn: U2. Admission charge

Prater Candy floss, balloons, carousels and an enormous big
wheel are the appeal of this fairground. Kids love to ride ponies,
test out the rollercoasters and bounce on the castles. ⓣ 0728
0516 ⓦ www.prater.at ⓔ info@wiener-prater.at ⓛ Amusement
park 10.00–01.00 Mon–Sun (Mar–Oct), closed Nov–Feb
ⓝ U-Bahn: U1 Praterstern

Schönbrunn Tiergarten Kids can smile at crocodiles, venture into
the Amazon rainforest and come eye-to-eye with polar bears

and pandas at the world's oldest zoo, set in the Schönbrunn Palace's grounds. ⓐ Maxingstrasse 13 ⓦ www.zoovienna.at ⓣ 01 877 9294 ⓔ office@zoovienna.at ⓒ 09.00–18.30 Mon–Sun (summer); 09.00–16.30 (winter) Ⓝ U-Bahn: U4 Schönbrunn. Admission charge

ZOOM Kindermuseum (Children's Museum) Tots can paint, dance and create music at this interactive museum. ⓐ Museumsplatz 1 ⓦ www.kindermuseum.at ⓣ 01 524 7908 ⓔ info@kindermuseum Ⓝ U-Bahn: U2 Museumsquartier. Admission charge

COMMUNICATIONS

Phones

Vienna's public telephones are easy to use and most have instructions in English. You can make international calls from any phone with coins or a prepaid phonecard (*Telefonkarte*), which you can purchase from a newsagent, post office or station. A handful of the city's internet cafés double as call centres and offer competitive rates for phoning abroad. Main post offices feature calling booths where you can speak in privacy. All mobile phones functioning on the GSM standard will be usable in Vienna.

Telephoning Vienna Dial 0043 for Austria, then 1 for Vienna and the five- to seven-digit number.

Telephoning abroad To call out of Austria, simply dial 00 followed by the country code and the local number.

National Directory Enquiries ⓣ 1151

International Directory Enquiries ⓣ 118811

Operator ⓣ 11816 or 11812

Post

Stamps are sold in post offices and some tobacconists. It costs €0.55 to send a standard letter or postcard to Europe (20 g) and €1.25 by economy airmail to North America, Australia, South Africa and New Zealand. Post boxes are bright yellow. Major post offices usually have ATMs and a bureau de change. Vienna's main post office on Fleischmarkt is open 24 hours a day. It's possible to locate branches online by entering the postcode. www.post.at

Internet

Internet cafés offering a high-speed, broadband connection have sprouted up all over the centre recently. Expect to pay between €3 and €6 for an hour online. Some cafés and bars with AOL terminals offer free, limited access for customers, including Restaurant Leupold on Schottengasse and Flex café near the Augartenbrücke. Try the following:

Big Net Has 18 terminals equipped with MS Office. ⓐ Hoher Markt 8 🕾 01 533 2939 Ⓦ www.bignet.at
ⓔ hohermarkt@bignet.at 🕓 10.00–24.00 Mon–Sun

Café Stein This arty Viennese haunt doubles as a relaxed internet/WiFi café where you can surf till the wee hours.
ⓐ Währinger Strasse 6–8 🕾 01 31972 41 Ⓦ www.café-stein.com ⓔ café-stein@café-stein.com 🕓 07.00–01.00 Mon–Sat, 09.00–01.00 Sun Ⓝ U-Bahn: U2 Schottentor

Speednet Café This chain of ultramodern internet cafés has some of the quickest connections in town. Find others at

Morzinplatz and Westbahnhof. ⓐ Europaplatz 1 ☎ 01 892 5666
ⓦ www.speednet-café.com ⓔ office@speednet-café.com
Ⓝ U-Bahn: U3 Stubentor

WiFi hotspots

Vienna is wising up to wireless internet access (wi-fi), with a
plethora of cafés, restaurants, bars, hotels and even petrol
stations offering the service. Some places offer free access
for customers, including Café Florianihof (Florianigasse 45),
Café Standard (Margaretenstrasse 63) and Levante (Mariahilfer
Strasse 88a). Other hotspots are:

Am Graben ⓐ Stephansplatz
Bar Italia ⓐ Mariahilfer Strasse 19–21
Café Central ⓐ Herrengasse 14
Donauturm Restaurant ⓐ Donauturmstrasse 4
MAK Café ⓐ Stubenring 5
Westbahnhof ⓐ Bahnhof Wien West

ELECTRICITY

Austria has a very reliable electricity system. It is 220 volts,
50 hertz (using round two-pin plugs).

TRAVELLERS WITH DISABILITIES

Vienna has made leaps and bounds recently in catering to
travellers with disabilities. You'll find many of the city's key
attractions are wheelchair-friendly and feature accessible
toilets, elevators and ramps. These include the Albertina, the
Belvedere, the Burgtheater (with dedicated spaces in the

auditorium), the Hofburg and the MuseumsQuartier. Most offer concessions (*Ermässigung*) for visitors with disabilities.

Featuring accessible toilets, the best restaurant choices for travellers with disabilities include Barbaro (Neuer Markt 8), Sacher (Philharmonikerstrasse 4) and Schweizerhaus (Prater).

For further information, consult one of the following:

Austria
BIZEPS @ Kaiserstrasse 55, Vienna ☎ 01 523 8921
Ⓦ www.bizeps.or.at @ zusendung@bizeps.or.at

United Kingdom and Ireland
British Council of Disabled People (BCDP) ☎ 01332 295551
Ⓦ www.bcodp.org.uk @ general@bcodp.org.uk

USA and Canada
Society for Accessible Travel & Hospitality (SATH) @ 347 Fifth Ave, New York ☎ 212 447 7284 Ⓦ www.sath.org
Access-Able Ⓦ www.access-able.com

Australia and New Zealand
Accessibility Ⓦ www.accessibility.com.au
Disabled Persons Assembly @ 04 801 9100 Ⓦ www.dpa.org.nz

FURTHER INFORMATION
Vienna Tourist Board
Vienna's English-speaking tourist board is located near the Opera House and provides information, maps and timetables, plus an accommodation and ticket booking service. There are

further tourist information desks opposite baggage reclaim at
Vienna International Airport and Westbahnhof station.
ⓐ Albertinaplatz/Maysedergasse ☏ 01 24 555 🖷 01 24 555 666
ⓦ www.wien.info ⓔ info@wien.info 🕐 09.00–19.00 Mon–Sun

Austria National Tourist Office
This well-illustrated and comprehensive site presents a wealth
of information on Austria. Browse for places to stay, themed
holidays, sights and attractions, restaurants, events and maps.
Brochures can be downloaded online. ⓦ www.austria.info

BACKGROUND READING

A Death in Vienna by Daniel Silva (Penguin). Discover more
about wartime Vienna in this thrilling novel which looks at the
relationship between the Catholic Church and the Holocaust.
Hundertwasser by Pierre Restany (Taschen). Dip into this book to
find out why wild child Hundertwasser's works and beliefs
made a splash on the Austrian art scene.
The Danube Cycle Way by John Higginson (Cicerone Press). Get
on your bike with this handy guide to cycling the River Danube's
well-marked trails. The book provides details on routes,
accommodation and attractions.
The Habsburgs: Embodying Empire by Andrew Wheatcroft
(Penguin). Tracing the rise and fall of the Habsburg empire, this
book is a fascinating insight into an incredible dynasty.
The Lonely Empress: Life of Elizabeth, Empress of Austria by Joan
Haslip (Weidenfeld & Nicholson). This biography takes a peek at
Princess Elizabeth's life – a bittersweet mix of romance and
tragedy which captured Austria's heart.

Emergencies

The following are national free emergency numbers:

Emergency services ℹ 112
Police ℹ 133
Fire ℹ 122
Ambulance & medical services ℹ 144
Emergency doctor ℹ 141
Breakdown (ARBÖ) ℹ 123

POLICE

Each of Austria's nine states has its own police force that deals with public security, traffic control and crime prevention. Like most other EU police forces, officers here wear navy blue uniforms and a white cap with a red-and-yellow trim.

MEDICAL SERVICES

It's advisable to have a valid health insurance policy before travelling to Austria. EU citizens are entitled to free or reduced-cost emergency health care with a European Health Insurance Card (EHIC). Pharmacies (*Apotheken*) are usually open 08.00–18.00 Mon–Fri and 08.00–12.00 Sat, but at least one in each district stays open 24 hours. For details on late-opening pharmacies, call ℹ 01 15 50 (recorded message).

If you need help finding an English-speaking doctor, contact the Vienna Medical Association Service Department for Foreign Patients ⓐ Weihburggasse 10–12 ℹ 01 501 512 53 (daytime); 01 513 9595 (24 hours). The doctors at Ambulatorium Augarten speak fluent English and the surgery accepts credit

cards 🖂 Untere Augartenstrasse 1–3 ☎ 01 330 3468
🌐 www.ambulatorium.com

The centrally located Vienna General Hospital (*Allgemeines Krankenhaus Wien*) provides emergency treatment 🖂 Währinger Gürtel 18–20 ☎ 01 404 000 🌐 www.akh-wien.ac.at

EMBASSIES

UK 🖂 Jauresgasse 12 ☎ 01 716 130 🕒 09.00–13.00, 14.00–17.00 Mon–Fri, closed Sat & Sun
USA 🖂 Parkring 12 ☎ 01 31339 7535 🕒 08.00–11.30 Mon–Fri, closed Sat & Sun
Australia 🖂 Mattiellistrasse 2–4 ☎ 01 506 740 🕒 08.30–16.30 Mon–Fri, closed Sat & Sun
Canada 🖂 Laurenzerberg 2 ☎ 01 531 38 3000 🕒 08.30–12.30, 13.30–15.30 Mon–Fri, closed Sat & Sun
Republic of Ireland 🖂 Rotenturmstrasse 16–18 ☎ 01 715 7698 26
South Africa 🖂 Sandgasse 33 ☎ 01 320 6493 🕒 08.30–12.00 Mon–Fri, closed Sat & Sun

---

EMERGENCY PHRASES

Help! Hilfe! *Heelfe!*   **Fire!** Feuer! *Foyer!*   **Stop!** Halt! *Halt!*

Call an ambulance/a doctor/the police/the fire service!
Rufen Sie bitte einen Krankenwagen/einen Arzt/die Polizei/ die Feuerwehr!
Roofen zee bitter inen krankenvaagen/inen artst/dee politsye/dee foyervair!

A

accommodation 37–41, 125–126

Aggstein 118

air travel 128

airports 50–51, 128

Albertina 65

Allander Tropfsteinhöhle 105

Ambrosi, Gustinus 93

Architekturzentrum Wien 80

arts see culture

Atelier Augarten 96

Augarten 90

B

balls 10, 12–15

banks 130, 131

bars, clubs & pubs 31–32, 73–74, 89, 102

Bermuda Triangle 31–32

boat travel 90–91, 122

bungee jumping 36

bureaux de change 130

Burg Dürnstein 118

Burg Wildegg 105

Burgtheater 66

bus travel 51, 55, 129

C

cafés & coffee houses 27, 28–29, 48, 70–72, 84–86, 99–100, 114–115, 124

campsites 37

car hire 58

children 82, 92, 132–133

city centre 60–75

concessions 54

crime 54, 131

culture 10, 11, 12–15, 20–22, 31, 33, 49, 65–69, 76, 80–82, 93, 96–98, 112, 120–121

customs & duty 129–130

cycling 34, 110, 122

D

dance 10, 12–15

disabilities, travellers with 135–136

Donauwalzerhaus 96

Dreidärrischenhöhle 108

driving 51, 58, 128

Dschungel Wien 80

E

electricity 135

embassies 139

emergencies 138–139

entertainment 31–33 see also nightlife

events 10–15, 47

F

Ferris wheel 94

festivals 11–12, 47

Föhrenberge Nature Reserve 108

food & drink 25–30, 69–70, 98–99, 113, 120, 122, 123

football 34

G

Gemütlichkeit 18

guesthouses 38–40

H

Habsburg Empire 16, 60, 109, 119

Halle E & G 80

Haus der Musik 66

health 130–131, 138–139

Heiligenkreuz 109

Heurigen 32

history 16–17
Hofburg 60
hostels 38
hotels 40–41
Hundertwasser, Friedensreich 91, 94, 96
Hundertwasserhaus 91

I

insurance 130–131, 138
internet 134–135

J

Jagdschloss Mayerling 109
Jüdisches Museum 66

K

Klosterneuburg 109
Krems Kunstmeile 120
Kunsthalle Wien 81
KunstHausWien 96–97
Kunsthistorisches Museum 66–67

L

Lainzer Tiergarten 112–113
Landstrasse 90–102
language 25, 30, 58, 139
Leopold-Figl-Warte 110
Leopold Museum 81
Leopoldstadt 90–102
lifestyle 18–19

M

MAK 67
malls 24, 48–49
Maria Taferl Basilica 118–119
markets 25–26, 27, 98–99
metro 55
money 130, 131
MUK 97

MUMOK 81–82
MuseumsQuartier 76
music 10, 11–15, 20, 66, 74–75, 89, 102

N

Naturhistorisches Museum 132
Neubau 76–89
nightlife 31–33, 72–74, 86–89, 100–102,
    115–116, 124–125

O

opening hours 22, 24, 131
Österreichische Galerie Belvedere 97
Österreichische Nationalbibliothek
    67

P

parks & green spaces 34, 47, 65, 90,
    95, 104–105, 108, 110, 112–113, 117,
    119–120, 122
passports & visas 129
pharmacies 130, 138
phones 133
picnics 28
Planetarium 97
police 138
post 131, 134
Prater 94, 132
public holidays 13
public transport 51, 54–57, 129

Q

quartier21 76

R

rail stations 51
rail travel 51, 129
Rathaus 61
regional Vienna 106–107

restaurants 27, 30, 71, 72, 74, 86–88, 100–102, 115–116, 124–125

Ringstrasse 61, 64

rollerskating 34–35

Römermuseum 120

Römertherme Baden 113

S

Sacher 71

safety 54, 130, 131

Sandstein Nature Reserve 110

Schatzkammer 67–68

Schloss Artstetten 119

Schmetterlingshaus 64

Schönbrunn Palace 49

Schönbrunn Tiergarten 132–133

seasons 10

Seegrotte Hinterbrühl 111

shopping 24–26, 27, 48–49, 69–70, 82–84, 98–99, 114, 123, 131

Spanischehofreitschule 64

spas & baths 36, 113

Spittelberg 76

sport & activities 34–36, 110, 113, 122

Staatsoper 68–69

Stadttheater Baden 112

Steinwandklamm 111–112

Stephansdom 64–65

Stift Göttweig 119

Stift Melk 119–120

Strauss, Johann 96

swimming 34

T

Tanzquartier Wien 82

Tausend-Eimer Berg 120

taxis 58

theatre 20, 80

Thermalbad Bad Vöslau 113

time differences 50

tipping 29

toilets 132

tourist information 33, 136–137

tours 90–91, 113–114, 122

tram travel 55

U

University of Vienna Botanical Gardens 95

V

Via Sacra trail 110

Volksgarten 65

Volkstheater 82

W

Wachau Valley 117–126

walking & hiking 34, 110

weather 10, 48–49

Weinstadtmuseum Krems 121

Weinstrasse Thermenregion 113–114

Wiener Konzerthaus 98

Wienerwald 104–116

Wienerwaldmuseum 112

wine 113–114, 120, 122, 123

Z

zoo 132–133

ZOOM Kindermuseum 82, 133

SPOT A CITY IN SECONDS

This great range of pocket city guides will have you in the know in no time. Lightweight and packed with detail on the most important things from shopping and sights to non-stop nightlife, they knock spots off chunkier, clunkier versions. Titles include:

Amsterdam	Bratislava	Glasgow	Madrid	Salzburg
Antwerp	Bruges	Gothenburg	Marrakech	Sarajevo
Athens	Brussels	Granada	Milan	Seville
Barcelona	Bucharest	Hamburg	Monte Carlo	Sofia
Belfast	Budapest	Hanover	Munich	Stockholm
Belgrade	Cardiff	Helsinki	Naples	Strasbourg
Berlin	Cologne	Hong Kong	New York	St Petersburg
Bilbao	Copenhagen	Istanbul	Nice	Tallinn
Bologna	Cork	Kiev	Oslo	Turin
	Dubai	Krakow	Palermo	Valencia
	Dublin	Leipzig	Palma	Venice
	Dubrovnik	Lille	Paris	Verona
	Dusseldorf	Lisbon	Prague	Vienna
	Edinburgh	Ljubljana	Porto	Vilnius
	Florence	London	Reykjavik	Warsaw
	Frankfurt	Lyon	Riga	Zagreb
	Gdansk		Rome	Zurich
	Geneva			
	Genoa			

The publishers would like to thank the following organisations for providing their copyright photographs for this book: Fotozentrum Reiberger page 14; Erik Holan/KunstHausWien page 99; Pictures Colour Library pages 13, 45 & 48; World Pictures pages 19 & 73; all the rest Caroline Jones. The author would like to thank Andy Christiani for his research.

Copy editor: Rebecca McKie
Proofreader: Ian Faulkner

Send your thoughts to
books@thomascook.com

- **Found a great bar, club, shop or must-see sight that we don't feature?**

- **Like to tip us off about any information that needs updating?**

- **Want to tell us what you love about this handy little guidebook and more importantly how we can make it even handier?**

Then here's your chance to tell all! Send us ideas, discoveries and recommendations today and then look out for your valuable input in the next edition of this title. As an extra 'thank you' from Thomas Cook Publishing, you'll be automatically entered into our exciting prize draw.

Send an email to the above address (stating the book's title) or write to: CitySpots Project Editor, Thomas Cook Publishing, PO Box 227, The Thomas Cook Business Park, Unit 18, Coningsby Road, Peterborough PE3 8SB, UK.